MW01028012

LAKE WASHINGTON
130 HOMES

A Guided Tour of The Lake's Most Magnificent Homes

David C. Dykstra

- Easy to follow maps
- Photos of each home
- Values and statistics
- Residents' Information
- Homes – Present or Past – of Bill Gates, Paul Allen, Craig McCaw, Barry Ackerley, Howard Schultz, Mike Holmgren, Detlef Schrempf, Rashard Lewis
  + 100 more multimillionaires

Hundred Homes Publishing
www.hundredhomes.net

ISBN-13: 978-0-9840591-0-2
ISBN-10: 0-9840591-0-5

```
728.809797 DYKSTRA 2009

Dykstra, David C.

Lake Washington
```

Library Resource Center
Renton Technical College
3000 N.E. 4th Street
Renton, WA 98056

Published by:
>	Hundred Homes Publishing
>	7683 SE 27th St. #170
>	Mercer Island, WA 98040
>	www.hundredhomes.net

Printed in the United States

**LIMIT OF LIABILITY/DISCLAIMER OF WARRANTY: THE
PUBLISHER AND AUTHOR MAKE NO REPRESENTATIONS OR
WARRANTIES WITH RESPECT TO THE ACCURACY OR
COMPLETENESS OF THE CONTENTS OF THIS WORK. THIS WORK
IS SOLD WITH THE INTENT IT WILL NOT BE USED FOR ANY
DECISIONS AND NEITHER THE PUBLISHER NOR THE AUTHOR
SHALL BE LIABLE FOR DAMAGES ARISING HEREFROM.**

ISBN-13: 978-0-9840591-0-2
ISBN-10: 0-9840591-0-5

Library of Congress Cataloguing-in-Publication Data

Dykstra, David C. 1941-
>	Lake Washington 130 Homes / David C. Dykstra

1. David C. Dykstra
2. Title
3. Travel – US – West – Pacific Northwest – Washington – Lake
    Washington – Seattle – Bellevue – Mercer Island – Medina –
    Hunts Point – Yarrow Point
4. House and Home – General – Pacific Northwest – Washington
    – Lake Washington – Seattle – Bellevue – Mercer Island –
    Medina – Hunts Point – Yarrow Point
5. History – US – Pacific Northwest – Washington – Lake
    Washington – Seattle – Bellevue – Mercer Island – Medina –
    Hunts Point – Yarrow Point

Library of Congress Control Number: 2009929895

Cover Photograph: Lake Washington from Mercer Island

Lake Washington Tour Map and Highlights

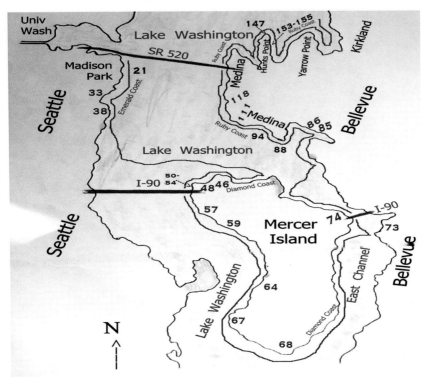

Map not to scale. ▬▬▬ Tour Route.

Page Numbers – Present and Past Residents/Owners:

21 – **Howard Schultz**, Starbucks Founder, SuperSonics Co-Owner; **33** – **Barry Ackerley**, Communications, SuperSonics Co-Owner; **38** – **Keith McCaw** (1953-2002), McCaw Cellular, Philanthropist; **46** – $35 Million For Sale; **48** – MI's newest $15 Million Mansion; **50-54** – 3 new $10 Million Mansions & **Kazuhiro Sasaki**, Mariners MLB star; **57** – $24 Million For Sale; **59** – $32 Million For Sale, Under Construction; **64** – **Paul Allen**, Microsoft Co-Founder; **67** – **Mike Holmgren**, Seahawks NFL coach; **68** – Southpointe, Amazon Executive; **73** – $9 Million For Sale, Newport Shores; **74** – **Rashard Lewis**, SuperSonics NBA star; **85-86** – **Detlef Schrempf** & **Jack Sikma**, SuperSonics NBA stars; **88** – $34 Million For Sale, Groat Point; **94** – **Charles Simonyi**, The "**Windows 2000 House**"; **111** – $45 Million For Sale, 1999; **118** – **Bill Gates**, Microsoft Co-Founder; **147** – $22.8 Million Lot For Sale; **153-155** – **Steve Ballmer**, Microsoft CEO; **Craig McCaw**, Cellular Phone Pioneer; and **Kenny G**, Saxophonist.

Thank You

Thank You Homeowners

These are the homes of the pillars of our community. These people are our area's leading professionals, business leaders and celebrities. They have built or extensively contributed to the area's skyline, factories, office parks, museums, theaters, zoo, medical facilities, and schools. Their trophy homes are showplaces of success. They have generously contributed to the region's and the world's non-profit organizations. Many have established family charitable foundations. Our narratives of the homes highlight these public charitable activities.

Public tours of most metropolitan mansions and estates are by road and the views are gates and protective trees and shrubs. The owners and residents of our one hundred thirty homes have shared the beauty of their homes and estates for public view from Lake Washington. The author, publisher and readers of this book thank these wonderful leaders for their success and contributions, and for sharing them with us.

Windows 2000 House – Charles Simonyi – page 94

Table of Contents

Preface

I moved to the Seattle area in 1994 from Newport Beach, California. I met my wonderful wife, Susan, and we were married in 2001. She has lived on Mercer Island waterfront for thirty-five years which is where we reside.

I previously enjoyed cruising Newport Bay and a major delight was seeing the mansions that graced the shores. I remember often seeing John Wayne and other celebrities on their docks waving to the boating passersby. I have transferred my cruising enthusiasm to Lake Washington which I enjoy even more because of the beauty of the lake's immense natural setting and wonderful large estates. In 1998 I remember seeing Bill Gates with his new child in his arms standing on his dock and he friendlily waved to us as we cruised by. Unfortunately, since 9/11 cruisers rarely see celebrity waterfront residents. We still enjoy seeing their homes and estates.

During our cruises there are always discussions about the homes and who lives there. A lot of my friends are knowledgeable but their information is limited and sometimes based upon secondary sources. My friends and relatives would often say, "There should be a guide book about these homes' physical statistics and history plus information regarding the present and past residents and owners." I was challenged, since I am a writer and photographer, to research the public information and produce such a book. I accepted this challenge.

As I delved into the project I found many intriguing stories. The reviewers of the first drafts commented, "Your statistics, current information, history and stories of the homes, their residents and the surrounding areas is fascinating reading for almost anyone – not just the lake's boaters and cruisers. And your photographs bring all your written words to life." I have expanded my initial scope to offer a book in a style that has never been used and will be interesting to a wide audience.

David Dykstra

Lake Washington and Its Homes

Lake Washington is the most beautiful large lake in the center of a major US metropolitan area. It is the second largest natural lake in Washington (Lake Chelan is the largest). Lake Washington was glacier carved, creating a long lake with steep hills on its shores with an average depth of 100 feet and a maximum depth of 214 feet. The water is clean as it is fed, primarily through the Cedar and Sammamish Rivers, with fresh rain and snowmelt from the Cascade foothills. The water flows out through the Lake Washington Ship Canal and the Ballard (Crittenden) Locks, Dam and fish ladders. The locks and dam control the lake's water level and allow large ships to pass from the lake's fresh water to Puget Sound and on to the straits and inlets of Canada and the Pacific Ocean.

Lake Washington is twenty-two miles long with over 130 miles of waterfront property on its shores and Mercer Island. The lake's waterfront offers fantastic views in all directions. Many western views are of the Seattle skyline with the Olympic Mountains in the background and include fabulous sunsets. Many eastern views are of the Bellevue skyline with the Cascade Mountains in the background. Southern views may include majestic 14,000 foot Mount Rainier. Looking north one can see an expanse of the lake, green hills and Mount Baker in the distance. Waterfront residents enjoy these views along with fresh water lake activities. In the summer, when the water surface temperature is in the mid seventies, the lake is dotted with swimmers, kayakers, yachts, sailors, parasailors, small pleasure and fishing boats, water skiers and personal watercraft (jet skis and their larger brethren). Because of the lake's large size it is rarely crowded.

Blue Angels flying over Lake Washington

Introduction

Lake Washington is famous for Seattle's **Seafair** summer celebration. This is a month long festival of many activities throughout Seattle and ends the first Sunday in August. The final four days feature hydroplane races and the Navy's Blue Angels' air shows. The hydroplane races are on the lake south of the I-90 floating bridge. The air show's center is this area. The planes and their stunts can be seen from much of the lake and its shores. During these four days the lake is crowded with spectator boats and the lake is renowned for the associated "floating party."

Seafair Party Time

Seafair hydroplane races

The **University of Washington** is on the lake just north of the 520 floating bridge. Many fans go to the UW Huskies home football games by boat and have tailgate parties on the water.

University of Washington Husky Stadium

Waterfront residents enjoy the above activities with their watercraft. They can keep large yachts in fresh water at their docks, cruise in the spectacular lake and continue to the salt water and its virtually unlimited destinations. Personal seaplanes also provide transportation. Lakefront residents enjoy a short commute to the downtowns of Seattle and Bellevue or the numerous nearby factories, office parks, medical facilities and the University of Washington – and they have their evening and weekend lake retreat. It is no wonder this property is so desirable!

In May 2009 there were eleven single family residences for sale with asking prices greater than $9 million in the Seattle area. All of them are Lake Washington waterfront properties and are on our tour. All of the area's members of *Forbes'* 2008 list of "The 400 Richest Americans" are on our tour.

The two **floating bridges** crossing Lake Washington were built in 1940 and 1963 and promoted development of Mercer Island and the area east of the lake known as "**The Eastside**." The first span of the floating bridge connecting **Seattle to Mercer Island** was built in 1940. The second span, as part of the Interstate Highway system (I-90), was completed in 1989. I-90 continues to the eastern mainland from Mercer Island via a conventional high-rise bridge. The 1963 (state route) 520 bridge, formally "The Evergreen Point Floating Bridge," at 7,578 feet, is the longest floating bridge in the world. It has a midsection that opens to allow the passing of large ships and barges. This bridge connects **Seattle to Medina** and points east.

Introduction

Our tour of 130 waterfront estates takes us along thirty miles of the lake's shoreline. Some estates have multiple homes, including 5,000 sq ft guest houses and an 11,000 sq ft separate home for mom, and one estate's lot is vacant and ready for a new house.

We start our tour at the 520 bridge on the eastside of Seattle where many of the city's wealthy resided in the 1800s and early 1900s prior to the floating bridges across the lake. This waterfront continues to be prime Seattle real estate with some of the old mansions along with new ones. I named this the "**Emerald Coast**" of the Emerald City, Seattle's official nickname.

Judge **John J. McGilvra** was the pioneer-founder of this area, **Madison Valley**, in the 1860s and a street is named after him. This waterfront is now home to: **Barry Ackerley**, former co-owner of the Seattle SuperSonics and former Chairman/CEO of The Ackerley Group (communications); **Howard Schultz**, the Chairman/CEO of Starbucks and the other former major co-owner of the Seattle SuperSonics; and actor **Tom Skerritt**.

We continue to **Mercer Island**, the "**Diamond Coast**" of the diamond in Lake Washington. One of Mercer Island's common nicknames is "The Rock." This is the largest and only residential island in Lake Washington. It is six miles long and averages about one mile wide for 6.4 square miles of land with about fifteen miles of waterfront. It has approximately 22,000 residents. **Paul Allen**, co-founder of Microsoft with Bill Gates, is the most famous Mercer Island waterfront resident. His numerous businesses include Vulcan Inc., Charter Communications, the Seattle Seahawks, the Portland Trail Blazers and the Seattle Sounders FC. For many years, he has been listed by *Forbes* as one of the wealthiest people in the world. **Mike Holmgren** lived on waterfront here when he was head coach of the Seattle Seahawks from 1999 to 2008. He was formerly the head coach of the Green Bay Packers and led them to the Super Bowl championship in 1997. **Jim Zorn** had a waterfront home here while he was quarterbacking the Seahawks from 1976-1984. He is now the head coach of the Washington Redskins.

We cross from Mercer Island to the "**Ruby Coast**" of The Eastside. This is locally known as the "**Gold Coast**" of Lake Washington. This overused moniker does not do justice to the gemstone quality homes along its shoreline. This coast includes part of **Bellevue** and the small exclusive communities of **Medina**, **Hunts Point** and **Yarrow Point**. The Ruby Coast covers about nine miles of shoreline including four bays and coves. This waterfront is a favorite of professionals, executives and business owners who work on The Eastside.

View of Bellevue from Groat Point in Medina

Bill Gates has the most famous waterfront home on this shoreline. He co-founded Microsoft with Paul Allen and is Chairman. He stepped down as CEO in 2000. Bill and his wife, **Melinda**, are co-chairs of the Bill & Melinda Gates Foundation. The Foundation has given charities over $20 billion. Some of the other notable Ruby Coast residents are: **Steve Ballmer**, CEO of Microsoft; **Jeffrey Brotman**, Chairman and co-founder of Costco; **James Sinegal**, President and co-founder of Costco; **Jeff Bezos**, President and founder of Amazon.Com; **Craig McCaw**, founder of McCaw Cellular and Clearwire Corporation; members of the **Nordstrom** (department stores) family; **Mark and Charles Piggot**, the current and previous CEOs of PACCAR; and **Kenny G**, the famous saxophone player, composer and songwriter. There is a vacant, except for a boat house, two acre lot with 748 feet of waterfront and 270° view for sale for $22.8 million!

The San Francisco Bay metropolitan area has its Silicon Valley of mansions and estates on hundreds of miles of roads where a tourist will mostly see protective gates, trees and shrubs. The Seattle/Lake-Washington metropolitan area has its Gemstone Waterfront Valley of mansions and estates on thirty miles of beautiful lakefront where boaters can view the prime side of the homes, grounds and waterfront.

Microsoft and Its Executives' Homes

Microsoft dominates our homes as it dominates the region's millionaires. 29 of our 130 estates are or have been the homes of past or present Microsoft executives. The company has created an estimated 12,000 millionaires, 1,000 with a net worth exceeding five million dollars and 4 billionaires. The early executives worked for low salaries and lots of stock. Microsoft rewards its employees with stock options.

The company started in 1975 and went public with its stock in 1986. Many of the early employees became millionaires with the IPO. The IPO price was $21 per share. The stock has split 9 times and is now, adjusted for those splits, worth more than 250 times its IPO price. At its 2000 peak it was worth more than 500 times its IPO price.

Microsoft co-founders, **Paul Allen** (page 64) and **Bill Gates** (page 118), were friends at Seattle's Lakeside High School. They were programmers using the Basic programming language and, working together, they built a computer. Paul graduated first in 1971 and went to Washington State University. Bill graduated two years later and enrolled in Harvard where he met **Steve Ballmer** (page 155).

Paul dropped out of college first and was working for Honeywell in 1974 when the first computer kit, the Altair 8800, came to market. He sold Altair on the idea of using Basic. Paul moved to Albuquerque in 1975 to work in Altair's headquarters as Director of Software. Bill dropped out of Harvard and joined him as Paul left Altair and the two formed a partnership named "Micro-soft."

The fledging partnership developed software. The partners moved to Bellevue in 1979, Ballmer joined them in 1980 and they incorporated in 1981 as Microsoft Corporation. A few weeks later IBM introduced its personal computer with Microsoft's MS-DOS 16-bit operating system. Microsoft's business virtually exploded.

In 1983 Paul was diagnosed with Hodgkin's disease and left the company to pursue less strenuous ventures. In 1986 Microsoft moved to its current main campus location in Redmond and issued its IPO. The company has expanded with Windows, MS Office, the Xbox, business software, development tools, and many more products.

Paul began building his Mercer Island compound (page 64) in 1985. Bill began building his Medina estate (page 118) in 1994. Steve (page 155) bought his Hunts Point estate in 1987 and remodeled it in 1991.

Estimated Values and Accuracy Disclaimer

The statistics and information in this book were obtained using public information posted on the Internet. Where possible items have been verified using multiple sources but I cannot verify or guarantee the accuracy of these sources.

The estimated values in this book are the author's estimates. An estimated value can be what a willing and qualified buyer would pay a willing seller. It can also be what it would cost to replace the home and its setting.

Each home in this book is unique. The features of each home and its lot are unique. Each home was custom built and has been upgraded to the owner's individual tastes. The value to the owners, therefore, may be substantially more than the market value. Less than ten percent of these homes sell each year because the owners have a customized dream estate fitting their individual personalities.

Estimates posted on the Internet are based on computer formulas and satellite images. Tax appraisal values are based on limited, and often incorrect, information and may not fairly value many intangibles. Detailed professional appraisals often change the previous public information that included square feet and number of rooms.

I have performed cruise-by estimates of each home. When I do a cruise-by estimate I carefully look at the amount and features of the waterfront and the views. These are extremely important in the value of waterfront-view property. The values of these are subjective, intangible and cannot be reasonably calculated by computer and satellite. I also look at the physical and architectural quality of the buildings and grounds. I have not inspected the buildings and grounds. I am not a professional appraiser.

If an estate was listed for sale in May 2009, I used the listing price for the value. If there was a recent sale-purchase I used the greater of that price or my cruise-by estimate.

The information, including the estimated values, in this book is not warranted for accuracy, is not intended for use for any decisions and should not be used for any decisions.

David Dykstra

Tour Information

The book provides a virtual tour or you may use it as a guide for a cruise-tour. You should allow at least three hours for a complete on-the-water cruise. You can start anywhere on a tour or in the book, go in either direction and take in as much as your time permits. I recommend you put a bookmark in the maps (pages 15-17, 40a, 40b, 80a and 80b) for reference as you read or cruise.

The information on the following pages is from public sources. The Internet is the primary medium but library books were used for some of the historical information. The bibliography is at the end of the book. The statistics that are shown for each estate are on pages 166-169 and explanations of each item are on page 169. The **maximum**, *minimum* and median for selected items are: value – **$150M**, *$3.5M*, $9.6M; water front feet – **748**, *42*, 138; sq ft living area – **56,660**, *3,670*, 7,950; and lot acres – **9.55**, *0.16*, 1.14.

I have included public information about the people who live or have lived in most of the homes. If the Internet political contribution websites show a pattern of contributions to a major party, I have noted that. Some owners have gone to great efforts to keep their names off public property information and news articles associating them with their homes. Some of the residents or owners have not significantly been in public news. In both cases I have classified the homes with "**undisclosed**" owners and residents and used the space to add photographs, trivia, information and history about the locations or previous owners.

Acronyms

Some of the acronyms used are: AFC – American Football Conference; ATP – Association of Tennis Professionals; B – billion; BOD – Board of Directors; CEO – Chief Executive Officer; CFO – Chief Financial Officer; COO – Chief Operating Officer; COB – Chairman Of the Board; EVP – Executive Vice President; GM – General Manager; HP – Hunts Point; I – Interstate; IPO – Initial Public Offering (of stock); LW – Lake Washington; M – million; MI – Mercer Island; MLB – Major League Baseball; MVP – Most Valuable Player; NBA – National Basketball Association; NFC – National Football Conference; NFL – National Football League; NHL – National Hockey League; PNW – Pacific Northwest; SR – State Route; SAM – Seattle Art Museum; UW – University of Washington; VP – Vice President; YP – Yarrow Point

Emerald Coast – Madison Park and Denny-Blaine

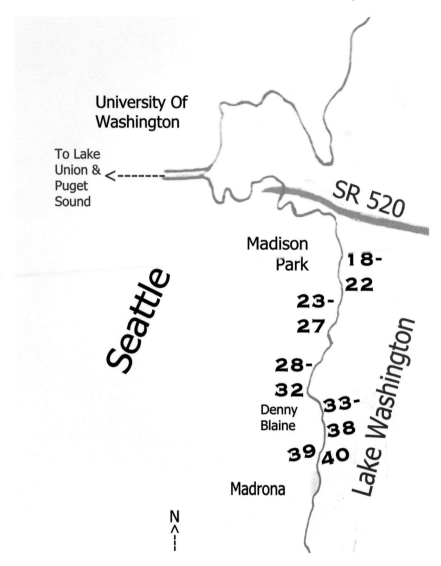

University Of
Washington

To Lake
Union &
Puget
Sound

SR 520

Madison
Park

18-
22

23-
27

28-
32

Denny
Blaine

33-
38

39 40

Seattle

Lake Washington

Madrona

N

Map not to scale
Numbers refer to page numbers

Diamond Coast – Mercer Island

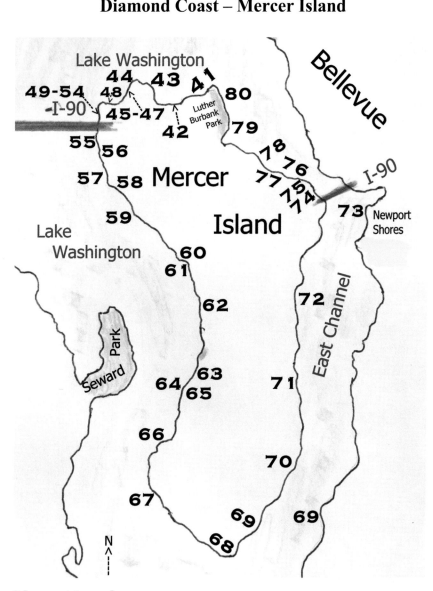

Map not to scale
Numbers refer to page numbers

Ruby Coast – Bellevue, Medina, Hunts Point and Yarrow Point

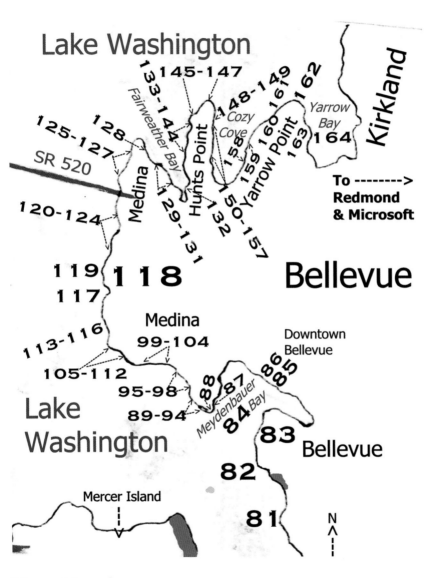

Map not to scale
Numbers refer to page numbers

Seattle
Madison Park – Washington Park Tower

This is the northeast-most point of our tour. We are just south of the SR 520 floating bridge looking at Seattle's Madison Park Neighborhood. The waterway connecting LW to Lake Union and the sound is northwest of the bridge. Lake Union has the most commercial marinas on LW to the locks waterways. Judge **John J. McGilvra** was the pioneer-founder of the Madison Park area in the 1860s when he acquired 420 acres. A street is named after him. McGilvra built a road through forest from Seattle to his property and named it Madison Street after **President James Madison**. McGilvra set aside 24 acres for a public park at the end of Madison Street. The neighborhood was the home of "Madison Park" and assumed the same name.

The 23 story Washington Park Tower is our landmark. The building has 53 condominiums and was built in 1969. This is the highest residential building on Lake Washington. It is very unlikely any more lake-front buildings close to this height will be built in the future because of zoning regulations. The residents enjoy incredible views. The three upper floors have two 2,200 sq ft, two bedroom units on each floor. The estimated value of each of these units is $2.2 million.

The Madison Park commercial district starts one block inland and covers about ten square blocks. It is an eclectic community of about 60 businesses including restaurants and coffee shops with sidewalk patio seating and various independently owned shops.

$12.9 million for sale listing (May 2009). 7,470 sq ft on 0.72 acres. 135 feet of waterfront, 6 bedrooms, 4.25 baths. Built in 1978.

This home features a pool, two kitchens and three fireplaces. The home is wonderful for entertaining inside and outside. Inside there are large entertainment rooms with French craftsmen detailing. The outside features the pool, beautiful, well-maintained landscaping, sculptures and fountains.

This is the home of **Jack and Carol Briggs**. They are real estate developers and philanthropists. They support numerous local charities and the arts. They are major supporters of the Governor's Mansion Foundation. They have hosted fund raisers in this home and the attendees have included governors and other luminaries.

$11 million estimated value. 9,000 sq ft on 1.0 acres.
136 feet of waterfront, 6 bedrooms, 8 baths. Built in 1936. Purchased in 1999 for $6.4 million.

This is the home of **Greg and Sharon Maffei**. Greg was with Microsoft as Chief Financial Officer from 1997 to 2000. He started with the company in 1994 and came from Citicorp as Vice President Venture Capital. He left Microsoft to join Seattle-based 360networks as CEO. In 2006 he became President and CEO of Colorado-based Liberty Media. The company is a $7 billion holding company with interests in communications and entertainment businesses. These include DIRECTV, Starz, Expedia, Time Warner and Nextel.

View of home in winter

View of home in summer

$30 million estimated value. 16,880 sq ft on 1.79 acres.
248 feet of waterfront, 4 bedrooms, 8 baths. Built in 1999.

This is the home of **Howard D. and Sheri Schultz.** Howard is the founder, chairman, president and CEO of Starbucks. The first Starbucks roasted and sold coffee beans and opened its first store in 1971. Howard joined the company as director of retail operations and marketing in 1982. In 1985 he founded a new coffee and espresso company which, in 1987, acquired the original Starbucks' assets and its name. Starbucks now has more than 15,000 stores throughout the world with $10 billion in annual sales. Howard is the former co-owner, with **Barry Ackerley** (page 33), of the Seattle SuperSonics of the NBA.

Howard has been nationally recognized for his philanthropic and educational efforts to battle AIDS. The Starbucks Foundation has given more than $11 million to more than 700 organizations. The Foundation's focus is improving the lives of youth through support of literacy and nontraditional education programs. The couple has contributed to Democratic candidates.

Moseley, Furman – Simpson Investment

$10 million estimated value. 7,360 sq ft on 1.2 acres.
134 feet of waterfront, 6 bedrooms, 5.75 baths.   Built in 1935.
Purchased in 1997 for $4 million.

This is the home of **Furman C. and Martha Reed Moseley**. Furman is the former president of Simpson Investment Company. He had been with the company for more than 35 years.

This home and the previous three (pages 18-21) are in an exclusive gated community of nine homes that are on the property of the **William Garrard Reed** (Martha's father) estate. He and his brother, **Frank**, were part of the Reed dynasty to run and transform Simpson Logging into the powerful and diversified **Simpson Investment Company** which is one of the largest privately-held corporations in Washington state. This company has been and continues to be a leader in the Seattle economy and local charities. Simpson was founded by **Solomon Grout Simpson** in 1890 and its first name was S.G. Simpson Company. The company started as a construction company and in 1895 got into logging and became Simpson Logging. In 1897 **Mark Edward Reed**, patriarch of the Reed dynasty, joined the company. Sol Simpson died in 1906 and Mark was named president in 1914 and started the company's diversification. Simpson Paper Company was formed. Mark's sons, William Garrard and Frank, started an acquisition program in the 1930s. Frank died in 1942 and William became the leader. (Continued on page 100 with his son, William G. Jr., and his home.)

The company now ranks as one of the largest forest products companies on the West Coast, one of the nation's largest producers of fine-paper and is diversified into plastics and other manufacturing.

$9 million estimated value. 6,420 sq ft on 0.41 acres.
120 feet of waterfront, 6 bedrooms, 3 bedrooms, 4.5 baths.
Built in 1960.

This is the home of **Joel and Julie Diamond**. Joel is Chairman and CEO of Diamond Parking. Joel is the son of **Josef Diamond** who was known in Seattle as the father of self-serve parking lots. Josef died in 2007 at the age of 99. Diamond Parking, founded by Josef's brother, Louis, in 1922 is the world's oldest parking company and operates over 1,000 locations throughout the western United States. Josef became CEO after WWII and led the major expansion of the company. Joel started with the company as a parking attendant in the 1960s and became CEO in the 1990s. Joel and Julie are the owners of Boatworld Marinas in Lake Union.

$8 million estimated value. 5,570 sq ft on 0.51 acres.
120 feet of waterfront, 4 bedrooms, 4.5 baths. Built in 1983. Purchased in 1992 for $3.0 million.

This is the home of **Dr. King K. Holmes** who heads the Infectious Disease Section at Harborview Medical Center and directs the University of Washington Center for AIDS and STDs. The Center was established in 2006 and the Bill and Melinda Gates Foundation (page 118) was the major donor. Dr. Holmes is a world leader in AIDS and infectious disease research and training and has won international and national awards for his accomplishments in these areas. He has been a UW faculty member for more than 35 years. He was also Chief of Medicine at Harborview in the 1980s.

The Seattle Tennis Club was founded a few blocks north of its present site as the Olympic Tennis Club in 1890. The name was changed to Seattle Tennis Club in 1896 and it moved to its current site in 1919. An $11.5 million renovation was completed in 1999. The club sits on 8 acres and offers its 3,000-plus members 19 tennis courts (including 6 indoor hard and 3 outdoor clay courts), a fitness center, squash courts, locker rooms, several dining rooms, banquet facilities, pool, beach, boathouse and pro shop. The club is popular for society wedding receptions.

Alvord, Ellsworth – Morgan Stanley, UW

$9 million estimated value. 5,895 sq ft on 0.8 acres.
100 feet of waterfront, 3 bedrooms, 3.5 baths. Built in 1972. Purchased in 1991 for $3 million.

This is the home of **Ellsworth C. and Eve Alvord**. He is with Morgan Stanley Dean Witter in their Seattle office. The **Seattle Center Eve Alvord Theater** is named after her. Ellsworth is the son of **Dr. Ellsworth "Buster" Alvord**, age 86, and retired from the University of Washington School of Medicine. The Alvord family members are well known Seattle area philanthropists, especially for contributions for multiple sclerosis research. Dr. Ellsworth was nationally recognized for his MS research. The family also gives generously to theaters, museums and the Woodland Park Zoo.

The Seattle Tennis Club is three properties north of this house.

$7 million estimated value. 5,220 sq ft on 0.68 acres.
120 feet of waterfront, 5 bedrooms, 5 baths. Built in 1910 and renovated in 1950. Purchased in 1999 for $4.2 million.

This is the home of actor **Tom Skerritt**. He has been in more than 40 movies and 200 television episodes. He won the Emmy for "Outstanding Lead Actor in a Drama Series" in 1993 for his role in *Picket Fences* as Sheriff Jimmy Brock. Some of his most notable movies are *M*A*S*H*, *Top Gun*, and *Harold and Maude*. His TV show appearances included *Cheers*, *Hawaii Five-0*, and *The Grid*. He has performed live at several Seattle theater-productions. He grew up in Detroit and, after spending a long time in Hollywood, was attracted to Seattle and moved here in 1987. His wife owns and manages a bed-and-breakfast on Lopez Island. He has contributed to Democratic candidates.

$9 million 9/21/2004 purchase price. 6,422 sq ft on 0.16 acres.
60 feet of waterfront, 3 bedrooms, 4 baths. Built in 1993.

This is the home of **Andrea Selig**. Andrea is the former wife of
developer Martin Selig (see next page). They separated in 1992. She
has contributed to Democratic candidates.

Kurt Cobain, a famous Seattle musician, rented a house a short distance
up the hill from here in the 1990s. He committed suicide in the house's
greenhouse April 5, 1994 and the greenhouse was torn down a few
months later. A bench in **Viretta Park** just south of here is host to a
makeshift shrine to Kurt. Thousands of fans of the music of Cobain's
band, Nirvana, have come here to pay tribute and guidebooks list the
park as the "Kurt Cobain Park."

$15 million estimated value. 8,690 sq ft on 0.44 acres.
180 feet of waterfront, 6 bedrooms, 6.75 baths. Built in 1981.

The home was listed for sale for a short period of time in 2007 for $27 million.

This is the home of **Martin Selig**. Martin is a major developer and operator of office buildings in Seattle. His projects include the tallest building in Seattle, the 76-story Bank of America (formerly Columbia) Tower. His company, Martin Selig Real Estate, has a portfolio of about 2.5 million square feet in Seattle.

$9 million estimated value. 4,020 sq ft on 0.59 acres.
153 feet of waterfront, 5 bedrooms, 2.5 baths. Built in 1925.

This is one of Seattle's fine old waterfront mansions that has not been torn down for a modern home.

This is the home of **Brooks S. Ragen**. He co-founded Seattle-based Ragen Mackenzie Group, a full service brokerage firm. The firm grew to 300 employees with offices in Washington, California, Oregon and Alaska managing over $11 billion in assets when it was acquired by Wells Fargo in 2000. Nearly simultaneously Brooks left the firm and co-founded McAdams Wright Ragen in Seattle and the firm is now one of the region's largest brokerage firms.

This home is in the **"Denny-Blaine Neighborhood"** that is immediately south of Madison Park. This area was developed in the early 1900s by **Charles L. Denny**, son of Seattle pioneer **Arthur Denny**, and **Elbert F. Blaine**; there is a Denny Blaine street. There are many magnificent old mansions up this hill overlooking the water.

$20 million 4/19/2000 purchase price. 7,010 sq ft on 2.59 acres. 60 feet of waterfront, 5 bedrooms, 3.75 baths. Built in 1929.

This is the home of **Russell C. Horowitz**. Russell is a founding executive officer, Chairman and CEO of Seattle-based Marchex, Inc. The company, founded in 2003, is a search and performance advertising company that uses innovative technology and techniques to connect businesses with potential customers in any local area. The company's products are used by more than 70,000 advertisers nationally. Russell was previously a founder (1996), Chairman and CEO of Seattle-based Go2Net, a provider of online services to merchants and consumers. Go2Net was acquired in 2000 by Bellevue-based InfoSpace (see page 95). He oversaw the successful completion of the merger and was President of InfoSpace until 2001.

Classic Mansion – Denny-Blaine, Seattle

$9.6 million for sale listing (May 2009). 7,990 sq ft on 0.44 acres. 63 feet of waterfront, 7 bedrooms, 5.5 baths. Built in 1910.

From the listing: "Idyllic waterfront home in prime neighborhood location. 1910 residence with gracious floor plan, elegant scale and classic detailing, such as covered terrace, french doors and windows, marble fireplaces, columns, cornice moldings, sconces and beamed ceilings. Gently sloping lawn to the water's edge and weeping willow tree. Dock with rare covered boat house and beach house with fireplace make for endless enjoyment of Lake Washington and all it has to offer."

$15 million for sale listing (May 2009). 6,580 sq ft on 0.46 acres.
146 feet of waterfront, 5 bedrooms, 4.75 baths.   Built in 1942.
Purchased 6/11/2008 for $13.3 million.

This was the home of **Barry and Ginger Ackerley**. Barry is the former
co-owner with **Howard Schultz** (page 21) of the Seattle SuperSonics
and former Chairman/CEO of The Ackerley Group.   The Ackerley
Group owned television and radio stations that were purchased by Clear
Channel Communications in 2001. Barry and Ginger head the Ackerley
Foundation. The Foundation's focus is early learning programs in the
Puget Sound region.

$8.5 million estimated value. 6,590 sq ft on 0.49 acres.
65 feet of waterfront, 7 bedrooms, 6.25 baths. Built in 1923.

This is the home of **Stuart M. Sloan**. Stuart was CEO of Bellevue based Quality Food Centers (QFC) from 1991 to 1996. Stuart was President and co-owner of Schuck's Auto Supply Inc. from 1967 to 1984. He and his partner, **Sam Stroum** (page 58) sold Schuck's in 1984 for about $70 million. He was a principal in Seattle-based Sloan, Adkins & Co, an investment firm, that bought QFC in 1986 and he became Chairman. At that time QFC was a privately held regional grocery store chain with 21 stores. QFC expanded, went public in 1997, was sold to Fred Meyer in 1997 and Kroger acquired Fred Meyer and QFC in 1998. Since then Stuart has been a philanthropist with a focus on reforming inner city elementary schools. One of his major beneficiary projects is Seattle's T. T. Minor public school.

$10 million estimated value. 7,060 sq ft on 0.76 acres.
120 feet of waterfront, 8 bedrooms, 8 baths. Built in 1932.

This is the home of **Richard J. and Bonnie Robbins**. Richard was President of Kent-based The Robbins Company from 1958 to 1993 when it was acquired by Sweden-based Atlas Copco AB. The Robbins Company (Richard is now a Director) invents, engineers, develops and produces tunnel boring machines. It now operates as a subsidiary of Atlas. Richard's father, James S. Robbins, founded The Robbins Company in 1952. Richard took over at the age of 25, two years after earning his engineering degree and upon the untimely death of his father. Richard and the company are noted for innovative designs that have enabled projects such as the English Channel tunnel and many aqueduct and hydro power tunnels. Richard holds 67 U.S. and foreign patents. He is now President of Seattle-based Robbins Group LLC which focuses on research and product development for The Robbins Company. In 2009 he received the Benjamin Franklin Medal in Engineering from the Philadelphia-based Franklin Institute.

Tong, Richard – Microsoft, Ignition Partners

$10 million estimated value. 10,390 sq ft on 0.72 acres.
100 feet of waterfront, 6 bedrooms, 6.5 baths. Built in 1905.

This is the home of **Richard C. and Constance Tong**. Richard is a founding partner, along with other former executives of Microsoft and McCaw, of Ignition Partners of Bellevue. Ignition started in 1999 and invests globally in emerging communications, Internet and software businesses and has become one of the largest venture-capital companies in the Northwest. Prior to starting Ignition he was with Microsoft for twelve years and was Vice President of Marketing for MS Office and BackOffice.

$20 million estimated value when complete – currently under construction. 13,300 sq ft on 1.0 acres.
160 feet of waterfront, 8 bedrooms, 12 baths.

This home is being built for **Bruce and Anne Blume** by Charter Construction. Bruce is a prominent commercial real estate developer. His firm, The Blume Co., is a major developer in the South Lake Union and University of Washington districts. He founded the company in 1982. The company owns 16 buildings on 10 acres in 6 centers. The centers are Yale Campus, 1100 Eastlake, Eastlake Center, University Center, 45th Street Place and Northlake Place.

McCaw, Keith (1953-2002) – McCaw Cellular

$35 million estimated value. 19,840 sq ft on 1.81 acres.
240 feet of waterfront, 6 bedrooms, 10.25 baths. Built in 1995.

This was the home of **Keith McCaw**. Keith tragically died at home of natural causes in 2002 at the age of 49. Keith and his three brothers, Craig (page 153), Bruce (page 106) and John (page 106), were pioneers in cellular communications. Please see page 152 for the McCaw family story. Keith had been listed by *Forbes* in its 2000 list as one of the wealthiest people in the world with a net worth of $1.6 billion. Earlier in the year of Keith's death, the four McCaw brothers gave $20 million to rename the Seattle Opera House after their mother, Marion Oliver McCaw Garrison. The Keith and Mary Kay McCaw Family Foundation has given millions of dollars to Seattle area charitable, educational and artistic causes. Keith was survived by his wife, **Mary Kay McCaw**, and their two daughters.

Madrona Neighborhood – Seattle

$11 million estimated value. 6,890 sq ft on 0.78 acres.
130 feet of waterfront, 3 bedrooms, 5.25 baths. Built in 1999.

South of the homes on this and the next page are Madrona Park and Leschi Marina. The park is run by the Seattle Parks Department and has 31 acres of woods, picnic areas, campground, a swimming beach and parking areas. It marks the transition from the Denny-Blaine Neighborhood to the Madrona Neighborhood which is named after the numerous madrona trees along the shore. The marina is modern, popular and has a restaurant area with guest docking. It is a popular lunch and dinner destination for Lake Washington boaters.

Madrona Park

Leschi Marina

Seattle
Rose, Peter – Expeditors International

$15.8 million 2/15/2008 purchase price. 9,200 sq ft on 0.46 acres.
120 feet of waterfront, 4 bedrooms, 8.5 baths. Built in 1930.

This is our southern-most Seattle home and is the home of **Peter J. and Patricia Rose**. Peter is the Chairman and CEO of Seattle based Expeditors International. *The Puget Sound Business Journal* named him "Executive of The Year" in 2004 and *Barron's* named him one of the top thirty CEOs of 2008. Expeditors is one of the largest global logistics companies with over 250 worldwide locations.

Emerald Coast – Madison Park and Denny-Blaine

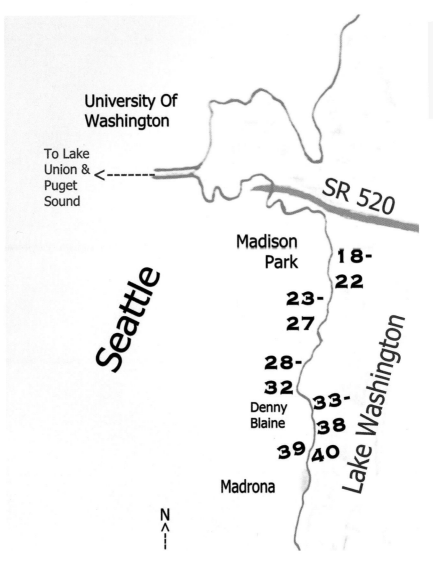

University Of
Washington

To Lake
Union &
Puget
Sound

SR 520

Seattle

Madison
Park

18-
22

23-
27

28-
32

Denny
Blaine

33-
38

39 40

Lake Washington

Madrona

N

Map not to scale
Numbers refer to page numbers

Mercer Island
Diamond Coast

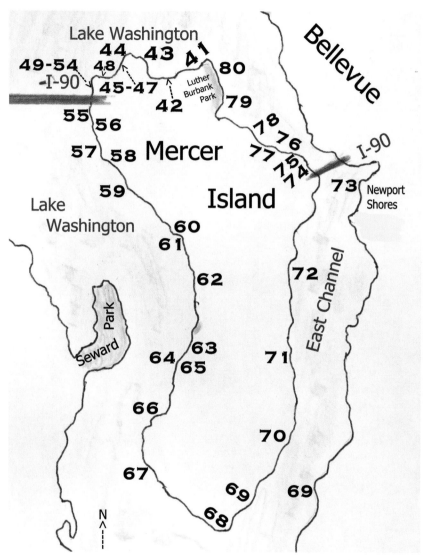

Map not to scale
Numbers refer to page numbers

Luther Burbank Park is on the northeast end of Mercer Island with spectacular views of Lake Washington. It is 77 acres with 4,000 feet of waterfront. Much of the park is undeveloped to foster a variety of wildlife. Amenities include a large children's play area, an off-leash dog area, group picnic areas, tennis courts, a public boat dock and fishing pier, a swimming beach with lifeguard and an amphitheater. The point is named **Calkins Point** after one of the first developers on the island (see page 55). (Continued on page 79)

$12 million estimated value. 9,360 sq ft on 1.6 acres.
145 feet of waterfront, 4 bedrooms, 4.75 baths. Built in 2006.

This is the home of a Microsoft software architect. The couple has contributed to Democratic candidates. This is our Mercer Island northeastern-most home west of Luther Burbank Park.

Higgins, Frank – Second Avenue Partners

$9 million estimated value. 6,990 sq ft on 0.9 acres.
160 feet of waterfront, 6 bedrooms, 5 baths. Built in 1990.

This is the home of **Frank M. II and Magid Higgins**. Frank (aka Pete) is founding partner of Second Avenue Partners in Seattle. The firm specializes in investing in and advising emerging Internet businesses. Prior to co-founding this firm he was with Microsoft from 1983 to 1999 in a variety of leadership and executive positions including a General Manager and Vice President position. He is Chairman of the Board of Kirkland based Market Leader, Inc. and is on the board of directors for Bocada Inc., Insitu Group and Advanced Digital Information Group. The couple has contributed to Democratic candidates.

$12 million estimated value. 10,580 sq ft on 1.2 acres.
132 feet of waterfront, 5 bedrooms, 6.5 baths. Built in 2001. Two lots and homes were purchased and the old homes were demolished to create the lot for this home.

This is the home of **Richard A. and Barrie Galanti**. Richard is with Costco as, since 1993, Executive Vice President and CFO. He joined Costco in 1984 as VP Finance. He has been a member of the Board of Directors since 1996. He was an Associate with Donaldson Lufkin & Jenrette Securities Corporation from 1978 to 1984. The couple has contributed to Democratic candidates.

See pages 90, 98 and 108 for more Costco information.

43

Dillon, Eric – Silver Creek Capital Management

$11 million estimated value. 7,960 sq ft on 1.3 acres.
210 feet of waterfront, 4 bedrooms, 4.5 baths. Built in 2001. Two lots and homes were purchased and the old homes were demolished to create the lot for this home.

This is the home of **Eric E. and Hollis Dillon**. Eric is a founding partner of Seattle based Silver Creek Capital Management, LLC. Silver Creek specializes in alternative investment strategies and has over $6 billion under management. Hollis is an attorney. Hollis and Eric are major supporters of the University of Puget Sound where Hollis received her undergraduate and law degrees. For the University, the couple established the Hollis and Eric Dillon Endowed Scholarship Fund and has been a major contributor to the science laboratory building and the new Center for Health Sciences. The couple has contributed to Republican candidates.

Mercer Island Information
Roanoke Landing and Tavern

Roanoke Inn and Tavern

The point where the home on the previous page is located is named **Roanoke Landing** and the western side of the point is where early 1900s mail and passenger ferries to and from Seattle docked. The landmark **Roanoke Inn and Tavern**, built in 1914, is one block inland. It was a popular spot as a watering hole for ferry travelers and an inn for island visitors. It looks today much like it did in the 1920s and is the oldest business on Mercer Island. It is no longer an inn but a very popular meeting place for the Islanders (moniker for people who live on the island). Many out-of-towners come to see it and have a meal and drinks.

The **City of Mercer Island** was incorporated in 1960. MI is the largest and only residential island in Lake Washington. It is six miles long and averages about one mile wide for 6.4 square miles of land with about fifteen miles of waterfront. It has 22,000 residents. It is the U.S.'s most populated island in a lake. Its school system has been ranked in the top five best in the state for many years and is often ranked number one.

Stanley Ann Dunham, mother of President **Barack Obama**, graduated from **Mercer Island High School**. Other notable graduates are: **Joel McHale**, comedian and host of television show, *The Soup*; **David Kirtman**, running back for the NFL's New Orleans Saints and former fullback for USC; **Quinn Snyder**, NBA Development League coach and former basketball star in high school and for Duke.

45

Lytle, Charles and Karen – Lytle Enterprises

$35 million for sale listing (May 2009). 22,779 sq ft on 2.0 acres. 150 feet of waterfront, 5 bedrooms, 9 baths. Built in 1977 and extensively remodeled and enlarged in 2000-01.

The home features a large indoor pool area with marble columns that is reminiscent of Las Vegas's Caesar's Palace. The mansion includes two fish ponds, two wine cellars, three kitchens and a mirrored gym.

This is the home of **Charles S. and Karen E. Lytle**. They are the founders of Leisure Care which they sold in 2003. They are the owners of Lytle Enterprises, founded in 1976, a developer and operator of retirement communities. The company has over 20 communities with more than 4000 residences in the western United States. Charles and Karen are active in numerous charities including Seniors Making Art, Performing Arts Center Eastside and Swedish Medical Center. The couple has contributed to Republican candidates.

The Lytles own another house, apparently for downsizing (page 157).

$11 million estimated value. 10,930 sq ft on 1.2 acres.
180 feet of waterfront, 4 bedrooms, 6.75 baths. Built in 1998.

This is the home of **George S. and Linda Suddock**.   In 1995 the
Suddocks moved from Alaska and purchased two lots and houses where
this house stands.   They had this house built and completed in 1998.
George has been Chairman of Alaska National Insurance Company since
1980 when the company was founded by George and other Anchorage
entrepreneurs. The company is headquartered in Anchorage and opened
a Seattle office in 1990. While in Alaska the couple contributed to and
supported charities, schools, hospitals and museums.   They have
continued their philanthropy in the Puget Sound region. The couple has
contributed to Republican candidates.

Mercer Island's Newest Completed Mansion

$15 million estimated value. 15,400 sq ft on 0.9 acres.
120 feet of waterfront, 8 bedrooms, 11 baths. Built 2007-08.

Two lots and homes were purchased and the old homes were demolished to create the lot for this home.

The home was featured in the Spring 2009 issue of *Luxe Magazine*.
The article describes the home as: "The owners, a young couple [he is a local real estate executive] expecting their first child, created . . . waterfront castle, independent guest wing, to cater to their exuberant entertaining. . . . a wine cellar . . . 1,700 bottles . . . 500 square-foot his-and-her walk-in closet, two offices, media room, eight-car garage. The great room . . . With its illuminated liquor cabinet, three Sub-Zeros and island-style table, the kitchen is the hub. . . . colossal yet cozy as a cocoon. . . . Graceful sprays of water arc from the fountain across the infinity-edge swimming pool." The home, of course, has incredible state-of-the art electronic controls, security and entertainment equipment throughout.

Faben Point – Mercer Island's Northwest Point

$10 million estimated value. 7,988 sq ft on 0.5 acres.
173 feet of waterfront, 6 bedrooms, 6.5 baths. Built in 2007.

This point is named after **Vince Faben**. He was an area pioneer who lived here in the early 1900s.

This is a picture from 2008 during construction of a house 2 houses east (upper left of top picture). Sometimes neighbors do not approve of new construction.

$9.3 million 8/14/2008 purchase price. 4,710 sq ft on 1.3 acres.
160 feet of waterfront, 4 bedrooms, 4 baths. Built in 1941.

Mercer Island is named after three **Mercer brothers**, Aron, Asa, and Thomas, from Illinois who migrated to the PNW in the 1850s and 1860s. Aron and Thomas came first, lived in Seattle and rowed to the island to hunt, fish and pick berries. None of the brothers lived or owned land on the island. The first federal survey in 1960 named the island "Mercer's Island." Asa came to the area after that. The brothers brought girls from the Midwest and East, known as "Mercer Girls," to marry PNW men. Thomas was the best known and was a Seattle judge and Seattle's Mercer Avenue and other landmarks are named after him. Mercer Slough in Bellevue is named after Aaron. The first white settlers came to the island in the 1870s. There were no Native Americans living on the island at that time.

$10 million estimated value. 10,340 sq ft on 0.7 acres.
90 feet of waterfront, 4 bedrooms, 5.25 baths. Built in 2005.

Around 1920 a Seattle land tycoon, **Sam Israel**, bought this parcel where three large mansions now stand (this and the next 2 pages). Sam lived here until 1961. After that his house was boarded-up and the weeds and blackberries grew wild. He died in 1994 at age 95 and his legacies are the Samis Foundation and the Samis Land Co. The Foundation is a major contributor to PNW Jewish schools.

The Foundation held this property and sold it to Bellevue-based Pacific Properties in 1998 and development plans began. The three houses were completed 2003-2006.

$10.4 million for sale listing (May 2009). 8,911 sq ft on 0.72 acres. 96 feet of waterfront, 5 bedrooms, 6 baths. Built in 2003.

From the Internet listing: "Exclusively Mercer Island . . . lakefront manse with suspended jewel box views dripping like diamond pendants. Impressive volume . . . negative edge pool . . . dancing under the stars in the el fresco party zone. A kitchen theater: beveled glass, commercial Viking range, dentil molding, Plasma TV. Sun Valley in Seattle ~ floor to ceiling river rock stone. Full home office; 3rd kitchen. Main floor master suite; full guest quarters. 96 feet of sandy beach. Gated shy suburban acre. Loge Seafair seats. Moorage."

This is the home of **John B. and Monica Norris** and their two children. John is the owner and CEO of Norris Homes Inc. Norris Homes, founded in 1991, builds homes in its 18 communities in the Puget Sound area.

$8.8 million for sale listing (May 2009). 9,000 sq ft on 0.76 acres.
110 feet of waterfront, 5 bedrooms, 9 baths. Built in 2006.

From the Internet listing: "One of a kind. 110' wft. Killer View West,
on MI's Faben Point with birds eye view of SeaFair. Commute to
Seattle or Bellevue in 5 min or downtown MI in seconds. Approx 9000
Sqft of living in main house plus separate guest house. Designed for
easy, relaxed living. Main level great room includes dual media perfect
for upscale entertaining or Super Bowl parties. Included in sale enjoy
the golf cart, 2 Supercharged SeaDoos and 25' Cobalt . . . Just bring your
Yacht! Truly designed for FUN!"

Sasaki, Kazuhiro – Mariners

$3.5 million estimated value. 3,880 sq ft on 0.43 acres.
85 feet of waterfront, 4 bedrooms, 2.5 baths. Built in 1996.

This is the former home of **Kazuhiro Sasaki** of the Seattle Mariners. He came from Japan and relief pitched for the Mariners from 2000 to 2003. He was a local icon. Fans cheered wildly when he came on in relief in the late innings of a close game. He had a repertoire of pitches but his most famous was a devastating split-fingered fastball that bounced and dropped in midair as it crossed the plate. It was legend and known as "The Thang." He was the 2000 season American League Rookie of the Year and an All-Star selection in 2001 and 2002. During his 3 seasons with the Mariners he pitched 129 saves. He longed for his home country and extended family and returned to Japan after the 2003 season. He pitched for two more years in Japan and retired from baseball in 2005 due to knee and elbow injuries.

The west coast of Mercer Island immediately south of the I-90 floating bridge is known as "**East Seattle.**" This area was settled in the 1880s and 1890s was the island's first large settlement. **Calkins Landing**, 0.5 miles south of the I-90 bridge, was the island's first commercial ferry dock, established in the 1890s. Prior to the bridges the housing in this area was mostly small cottages. Some of these early 1900s cottages remain within a few blocks of the water.

2009 Picture of early 1900s East Seattle Cottage

There were about 25 **ferry landings** around Mercer Island at the time the first East Channel bridge was completed in 1923. Most of the landings were for ferries that circled the island. Calkins Point (page 41) served Seattle to Mercer Island to Bellevue ferries. The other main Seattle to Mercer Island ferries landed at Roanoke Landing (page 45) and Calkins Landing in this area. The ferry for Mercer Island's children going to school across the lake docked on both sides of the lake about one mile south of the I-90 bridge. Ferries to Seattle continued until the first floating bridge was completed in 1940.

The south end of this shore and the homes on the next two pages are in the **Proctor Landing** area and directly across the lake from the **Stan S. Sayres** (page 147) **Memorial Park**, known as the "**Sayres Pits**" established in 1957. They are on the west side of LW south of the I-90 Bridge. The pits are the launching, service and staging area for **Seafair**'s hydroplane racing boats.

Jain, Naveen – Microsoft, InfoSpace
Facq, Jean-Remy – Microsoft, InfoSpace

$8.5 million estimated value. 10,700 sq ft on 0.43 acres.
80 feet of waterfront, 6 bedrooms, 8.5 baths. Built in 1995.

The Seattle Times reported March 6, 2005; this home was acquired by
Naveen Jain (page 95) from **Jean-Remy Facq** in 2005 in a private
transaction. According to the article Facq bought this house in 1999.
Jean-Remy, an engineer born in France, had worked with Naveen at
Microsoft. The two left the company in 1996 when Naveen founded
Bellevue-based InfoSpace, Inc., a provider of Internet services. Facq
was the company's chief systems architect. InfoSpace went public in
1998 and the stock soared to $1,000 per share. Naveen became a
billionaire, Jean-Remy became a multimillionaire and both went on a
spending spree. InfoSpace stock plunged to $3.90 in 2002 and Naveen
took over this house. Facq now runs a web site, facq.net, to distribute
software applications he has written. He has contributed to Democratic
candidates.

$23.9 million for sale listing (April 2009). The home may be in escrow as this book goes to press. 17,780 sq ft on 1.37 acres. 255 feet of waterfront, 8 bedrooms, 15 baths.

The original house was built in 1932. It was purchased in 1998 for $7.9 million and extensively expanded and remodeled, maintaining the original English Tudor architecture. The interior of the home has been described as a mini "Taj Mahal." The home features an indoor/outdoor pool, a two bedroom guest house, a children's room in the tower and a three office carriage house.

This is the home of **Jonathan D. Lazarus**, formerly with Microsoft as Vice President Strategic Relations. He retired from the company in 1996 at the age of 44. He joined the company in 1986 and he was responsible for the marketing introduction of Windows. Since 1996 he has worked as an investor and consultant with over twenty entrepreneurial Internet companies. He has contributed to Democratic candidates.

Glazer, Marsha – Philanthropist
Leven, Bruce – Bayside Disposal, Race Car Driver

$11 million estimated value. 11,300 sq ft on 1.01 acres.
244 feet of waterfront, 4 bedrooms, 5.5 baths. Built in 1995.

Marsha Sloan Glazer purchased this home in 2006 for an undisclosed amount. She is a prominent philanthropist and theater patron. She supports numerous causes financially and hosts fund raisers as a board member and trustee of many organizations. Her contributions include $1 million each to the Seattle Repertory Theater and Seattle Children's Hospital and Medical Center. She is the daughter of the late **Sam Stroum**, a prominent area philanthropist. Sam and **Stuart Sloan** (page 34) were former co-owners of Schuck's Auto Supply.

This was the home of **Bruce Leven** from 1992 to 2006. Bruce, born in 1939, was a race car driver, waste disposal tycoon and automobile dealership owner. He started his garbage business in 1964 buying a garbage truck in Seattle. In the 1980s his Bayside Disposal Company Inc. had 400 trucks in 10 locations. He sold Bayside to Illinois-based Waste Management Inc. in 1987 but continued in the waste management business and, in addition, started acquiring Puget Sound area automobile dealerships that included Bayside Porsche and Saab, Bayside Jeep Eagle and Bayside Toyota. He competitively raced Porsches.

$32 million for sale listing (May 2009). 13,636 sq ft on 1.67 acres. 160 feet of waterfront, 7 bedrooms, 12 baths.

Construction started in 2007. From the Internet listing: "Radiating life on a golden Northwest Island peninsula of choice sun burnished grounds! The strength of the framework reflects the passion for excellence that was demanded for the execution of this manse. The spirit of today ~ the intent of forever. A pavilion axis focuses on the breathtaking views and 164 footage of remarkable, wade-in lakefront. Epitomizing the incomparable concept of living to the fullest. The protection of a village acre."

This is the largest new home construction on Mercer Island in the 21st Century. Ben Leland Construction, a division of Hochanadel Homes, Inc., is the builder and **Todd Hochanadel** is the President/Owner of both companies. The company has built many custom homes in the Puget Sound area.

59

$7.5 million estimated value. 5,290 sq ft on 0.49 acres.
195 feet of waterfront, 4 bedrooms, 3.25 baths. Built in 1983. Sold by **Jim Zorn** in 1988 for $1.3 million.

Locals call this the "gingerbread house." Jim Zorn of the Seattle Seahawks built this home and lived here while he was quarterbacking the team from 1976-1984. He was the star quarterback for the expansion NFL Seattle Seahawks' first seven seasons. He was a young, charismatic leader and a fan favorite. After his first season he was named NFC Offensive Rookie of the Year and the team MVP. During his Seahawk reign he teamed with Hall of Fame receiver **Steve Largent**. Largent was the first inducted into the Seahawk "Ring of Honor" in 1989 and Zorn was the second in 1991. After the Seahawks he played for the Green Bay Packers, the Winnipeg Blue Bombers and the Tampa Bay Buccaneers. He was an assistant coach for 3 colleges from 1988-96 and 3 NFL teams from 1997-2007, including the Seahawks from 2001-07. He has been the head coach of the Washington Redskins since 2008.

Mercer Island Information
Seattle's Seward Park

$9 million estimated value. 8,170 sq ft on .94 acres. 210 feet of waterfront, 5 bedrooms, 6.25 baths. Built in 1948 and extensively remodeled in 1982.

View of Seattle's Seward Park from Mercer Island

Seward Park is southwest of this home. From here the park appears to be an island but it is connected to the mainland by a narrow isthmus and is part of the Bailey Peninsula. The park is 300 acres of old growth forest with eagles' nests, a 2.4 mile biking and walking trail circumventing the park, interior trails, numerous picnicking and play areas, an amphitheater, a native plant garden and an art studio. Andrews Bay is north of the isthmus and is a popular spot for anchoring, having boat parties and spending the night on summer weekends.

$9 million estimated value. 5,850 sq ft on 1.24 acres.
190 feet of waterfront, 5 bedrooms, 4.75 baths. Built in 2002.

This is the home of **Brad M. and Judy Chase**. Brad was with Microsoft as Senior VP of the Consumer Group. He spearheaded the launch of Windows 95 and the company's Internet push. He left the company in 2001 at the age of 40. He had been with the company since 1987. In 2006 he joined Vizrea, a startup providing digital media sharing, as Chairman. The Seattle-based company was created by former Microsoft executives, changed its name to WebFives and was acquired by Microsoft in 2007.   The couple has contributed to Democratic candidates.

$8.5 million estimated value. 5,400 sq ft on 0.87 acres.
200 feet of waterfront, 3 bedrooms, 3 baths. Built in 2003.

This is the home of **Joseph L. and Judith Schocken**. Joseph is president and founder (1987) of Broadmark Capital, LLC, a prominent Seattle investment bank. The firm has raised more than $1 billion for investment in 75 (and growing) regional businesses. Most of these are technology related and the investments can be for start-up or secondary stages. Bennett Environment, Optiva and Universal Access are some of the firm's client companies. Joseph is on the boards of numerous companies. He has been in the investment banking business for more than 30 years. The couple has been a top donor and fund raiser for the Democratic Party. Joseph is a member of the National Advisory Board of the Democratic National Committee. High level receptions for Democratic candidates have been held in their home.

Allen, Paul – Microsoft, Seattle Seahawks

<u>A</u> – 4 buildings ~200 ft from water: 10,680 sq ft main building with gym and 2 indoor tennis courts; 5,220, 4,210, and 2,050 sq ft guest houses; and 12+ car garages for an antique and race car museum and guest parking.

<u>B</u> – Mother's house, ~50 feet from water, 11,300 sq ft plus 7 car garage.

<u>C</u> – Catamaran, *Dragonfly*, to drag-and-fly helicopters.

$150 million estimated value. 56,660 sq ft on 9.6 acres.

505 feet of waterfront, 25 bedrooms, 28 baths. The campus includes multiple lots that were acquired starting in 1985. Building also started in 1985 and the estate is a constant work in process.

This is the home of **Paul G. Allen**. He is a co-founder of Microsoft (page 12) with **Bill Gates** (page 118). He is Mercer Island's most famous resident. His numerous businesses include Vulcan Inc., Charter Communications, the Seattle Seahawks, the Portland Trail Blazers and the Seattle Sounders FC. He has been listed by *Forbes* as one of the wealthiest people in the world with his 2008 net worth estimated at $16 billion. He created the Paul G. Allen Family Foundation in 1986. Personally and through the Foundation he has given over $30 million a year mostly to non-profit organizations in health and human services and for the advancement of science, technology and music. The Experience Music Project (EMP) at Seattle Center, next to Space Needle, was funded by Paul. (continued on next page)

D – Main house including attached indoor pool and lakefront building to the north and wood garden/lakefront house to the south, 9,890 sq ft.

E– Concert hall theater and guest facilities, 11,560 sq ft.

F – 1,750 sq ft house with 100 ft waterfront acquired in 2006 for $5.2 million.

(Continued from previous page) When the Portland Trailblazers, owned by Paul, were playing the Sonics in Seattle the team could stay in the compound and scrimmage in his NBA regulation-sized gym. When he dated Tennis Hall of Fame star **Monica Seles** she could work out with neighbor **Michael Chang** (next page) on the inside tennis courts.

A Mercer Island city street bisects the compound and the city would not permit Allen to build bridges over the street. His solution was he paid to have the road raised and constructed a tunnel under it and planted high hedges along its side. Most of the buildings are connected with tunnels.

The city also would not allow him to have a helicopter-pad or land helicopters within the shoreline. He solved this problem by purchasing the large catamaran, *Dragonfly* (C above), that motors 100 yards off-shore and his and guests' helicopters land and takeoff on it.

Chang, Michael – Tennis

$10 million sale 3/27/2008. 6,620 sq ft on 0.73 acres.
237 feet of waterfront, 5 bedrooms, 4 baths. Built in 1988.

This is the former home, sold in 2008, of tennis star **Michael Chang**. He holds the record for the youngest male to win a Grand Slam singles tennis tournament. He attained this record at the age of seventeen in 1989 when he won the French Open. He played for the US in Davis Cup matches and the Olympics. He was a top 10 ATP player for many years and was ranked number 2 at his peak. He earned over $19 million in prize money. He retired from professional tournament tennis in 2003 and was inducted into the International Tennis Hall of Fame in 2008. His brother, Carl, moved to Mercer Island simultaneously with Michael in the early 1990s. Carl, also an outstanding tennis player, was Michael's coach for many years. Michael and Carl worked out on the indoor courts at Mercer Island Country Club and played in local exhibition matches raising money for local charities.

$3.7 million sale 4/4/2008. 3,670 sq ft on 1.40 acres.
96 feet of waterfront, 4 bedrooms, 2.75 baths. Built in 1992. Although not much of the home can be seen from the water it is on a large lot and has a fantastic view of the lake and sunsets.

This is the former home of **Mike and Kathy Holmgren** that they sold in 2008. He was head coach of the Seattle Seahawks from 1999 to 2008. During his reign the Seahawks had 86 wins and 74 losses, 5 division championships and 1 NFC championship, losing to Pittsburg in Super Bowl XL. He was formerly the head coach of the Green Bay Packers and led them to the Super Bowl championship in 1997. He grew up in San Francisco (born 1948) where he played quarterback in high school. He went on to play back-up quarterback at USC, was drafted in the 1970 NFL draft but never played and started coaching in 1971. He moved up from the high school level through colleges to an assistant in the NFL at the San Francisco 49ers in 1986. He became head coach of the Packers in 1992. Mike retired at the end of the 2008 season and he and Kathy are building a new house in the San Francisco Bay Area.

$7 million estimated value. 5,150 sq ft on .63 acres.
147 feet of waterfront, 5 bedrooms, 4 baths. Built in 1990. Purchased 7/3/2007 for $5.6 million and it went through extensive renovation and upgrades in early 2009.

This is the home of **Marc A. and Sally Onetto**. Marc is Sr. VP Worldwide Operations for Amazon.Com (page 105). He joined the company in 2007. He was with Solectron Corp in California as Executive VP from 2003 to 2006, was with GE for 15 years and with Exxon for 12 years.

Amazon's 2006 revenues were $10 billion, they grew to $19 billion in 2008 and the June 2009 annual rate exceeded $25 billion. In 2006 the stock traded as low as $26 per share and in 2009 it has traded between $47.63 and $88.56 per share.

This property is a landmark known as **"Southpointe."** It is on the southern tip of Mercer Island and from here there are fabulous views of the lake and Mount Rainier.

Mercer Island Information
Parks, Clubs, Seahawks

Mercer Island Beach Club

Clarke Beach Park

Around the point and northeast of "Southpointe" (previous page) is the **Mercer Island Beach Club** and north of here is the 9 acre **Clarke Beach Park**. The 2 acre Beach Club is a member-owned private club and offers members tennis, beach and pool swimming, a clubhouse for club and private parties and boat moorage. The park offers picnicking, fishing and swimming.

The Beach Club and **Mercer Island Country Club,** up the road and inland, have very strong youth swimming and tennis programs and have rival inter club competition. Mercer Island High School is a perennial state power in swimming and tennis with many of the student stars coming from these clubs' programs. The girls and boys HS tennis teams have won 41 state championships.

Seahawks headquarters and practice facility

Looking east across the lake in Renton is the 19 acre Seahawks headquarters and practice facility which opened in 2008. The facility is state-of-the-art and considered one the NFL's top 3 team facilities. It has one indoor and four outdoor full-size football fields plus administrative offices, gyms, rooms for lockers, training, dining and conferences and a 146-seat auditorium. The buildings have 113,000 square feet.

$8 million estimated value. 8,400 sq ft on 0.62 acres.
95 feet of waterfront, 5 bedrooms, 6.25 baths. Built in 2003.

This is the home of **Richard Ferry**, retired Founder Chairman of Korn/Ferry International. Korn/Ferry is the largest and regarded as one of the most prestigious international executive search firms. Mr. Ferry co-founded Korn/Ferry with Lester Korn in 1969. Mr. Ferry retired in 2001 and moved from Los Angeles to Mercer Island because of his love for the Pacific Northwest. He purchased this lot and its old home for $1.6 million in 1999 and built this home in 2003.

This home is 10 houses north of Clarke Beach Park (previous page).

$10 million estimated value. 11,400 sq ft on 1.9 acres.
260 feet of waterfront, 5 bedrooms, 6.5 baths. Built in 1995.

This is the home of a couple who are private investors. He is a retired dentist from Bellevue. The couple purchased this lot and its old home for $2.4 million in 1993 and built this home in 1995. They purchased a second home in the Las Vegas area for $7.9 million in 2007. The couple has contributed to Republican candidates.

This area of Lake Washington is known as the East Channel. The home on the next page is one the old Mercer Island estates on a large lot and our northern-most Mercer Island home south of the I-90 East Channel bridge that connects the island to Bellevue. The first bridge here was completed in 1923 and provided the first road off the island. Estates were soon established in this area. The first bridge was torn down and one span of the current bridge was built in 1940.   The second span was opened in 1992 as part of the I-90 system.

Mercer Island
Humphrey, David – ILD Global
Bonica, John – UW

$8 million estimated value. 6,880 sq ft on 1.47 acres.
175 feet of waterfront, 6 bedrooms, 5.75 baths. Built in 1934.
Purchased 7/17/1996 for $2.6 million.

This is the home of **David R. and April Humphrey**. The couple co-founded ILD Global in 1995. David, a retired Medical Doctor, is President and CEO and April is VP. The company is a business development and consulting enterprise and conducts frequent business briefing seminars for independent business owners. The couple is actively involved in fundraising for the arts, charities and civic organizations. The couple has contributed to Republican candidates.

This is the former home of **John J. and Emma Bonica**. John, who died of a stroke at the age of 77 in 1994, was a world-renowned anesthesiologist and UW professor. He helped pioneer anesthesiology as a specialized field of medicine, was founder and chairman of UW's Department of Anesthesiology and published numerous articles and books on the subject.

This home is across the lake's East Channel from the home on the next page and our northern-most most home on Mercer Island south of the East Channel bridge.

$8.8 million for sale listing (May 2009). 7,360 sq ft on 1.17 acres. 210 feet of waterfront, 5 bedrooms, 5 baths. Built in 2002.

From the Internet listing: "Newport Shores premiere waterfront property. Custom, spectacular Jeff Loveless designed 7300 sq ft mansion captures sun rays horizon to horizon. Light filled grand entry hall and main living. Hand crafted clear fir and oak timbers of grand proportions. Spa and cabana adjacent to pool and expansive lawns. Seaplane lift. Ample moorage. Garages for eight. Designed to fully experience 1.17 acres and 210′ of waterfront."

We crossed from Mercer Island to Newport Shores on the Ruby Coast. Newport Shores is a Bellevue neighborhood built in the 1960s and consists of man-made peninsulas and canals. The neighborhood has 343 homes on 172 acres. 100 of the homes are on lake or canal waterfront. The Newport Yacht Club is located within the neighborhood and has a clubhouse, numerous amenities and a 119 boat slip marina.

Mercer Island
Lewis, Rashard – SuperSonics

$4.4 million for sale listing (May 2009). 8,000 sq ft on 0.41 acres.
85 feet of waterfront, 5 bedrooms, 4.5 baths. Built in 1990.

From the Internet listing: ". . . has been updated w/new finishes throughout. There's endless entertaining opportunities. Open gourmet kitchen/family room, large Master Suite w/glass atrium master bath. Upstairs guest or nannies quarter. Lake level game room, wet bar, movie theater, and sun room. Dock w/2 slips /2 jet ski lifts. A casual elegant life style throughout."

This is the former home of basketball star **Rashard Lewis**. He started his NBA career with the Seattle SuperSonics in 1998 and was one of their stars through the 2006-07 season. He averaged over 20 points per game each of his last three years with the Sonics. In a $118 million deal he went to the Orlando Magic where he has played for the past two seasons. During the playoffs ending June 2009 he was the team's number two scorer behind Dwight Howard and was a key player in leading the team to the NBA finals. He was selected for the NBA All-Star teams for the 2004-05 and 2008-09 seasons.

This is our southern-most most home on Mercer Island north of the East Channel Bridge.

$7.5 million estimated value. 3,950 sq ft on 0.58 acres.
112 feet of waterfront, 3 bedrooms, 3.25 baths. Built in 1990.

This is the home of **Frank A. Jr. and Charlene Blethen**. Frank is the Publisher and CEO of *The Seattle Times*. Frank's great grandfather, **Alden J. Blethen**, founded *The Seattle Times* in 1896 and Frank is the fourth generation of family leadership. Frank became Publisher in 1985 and the paper has received numerous awards, including three Pulitzer Prizes, under his leadership. The Blethens are involved in many civic activities and support many charitable causes. Their favorite causes are education, cultural diversity and health and human services.

$8.5 million estimated value. 9,150 sq ft on 1.0 acres.
100 feet of waterfront, 5 bedrooms, 4.5 baths. Built in 2002.

This is the home of **Jeffrey I. and Judith Greenstein**. Jeffrey was the Chief Executive of Quellos Group, a Seattle investment firm. He founded the firm in 1994 and it grew to become one of the world's largest fund-of-hedge-funds with over $17 billion in assets under management. Quellos's assets were acquired for $1.7 billion by BlackRock, Inc. in October 2007. New York based BlackRock is one of the world's largest publicly traded investment management firms. Jeffrey retired following completion of the acquisition. The couple has contributed to Democratic candidates.

Basketball
Covenant Shores – Retirement Community

Basketball legends, **Ed Pepple** and **Fred "Downtown Freddie" Brown**, live inland on Mercer Island. Ed is in the Washington state basketball Hall of Fame with the state's record high school coaching wins (952) over his 49 year coaching career with 43 years at MIHS. His teams won 4 state championships. He retired after the 2008-09 season. Fred Brown starred playing 13 seasons from 1971 through 1984 with the Sonics, scoring 14,018 points. He got the nickname "Downtown" for his outstanding three point shooting. He played on the 1979 NBA championship team with **Jack Sikma** (page 86). Fred's #32 jersey was retired by the Sonics. He had four sons who starred on MIHS's basketball team over a period of 12 years. Two of the sons were leaders on state championship teams.

Covenant Shores – Retirement Community

Covenant Shores consists of 9 buildings with 400,000 sq ft on 12 acres. The community is part of Christian based Covenant Retirement Communities. This parent company operates 14 communities in the U.S. from coast to coast. It started with an assisted living residence in Chicago in 1886 and pioneered continuing care retirement communities in 1951 in Florida. Covenant Shores opened in 1970 and averages 300 residents. It has independent apartment, assisted, memory support and skilled nursing living. Its facilities include a private marina, putting green, picnic and barbeque areas, health club, shops, barbershop, beauty salon, workshops, library, and dining, meeting and game rooms.

$9 million estimated value. 9,670 sq ft on 0.64 acres.
100 feet of waterfront, 6 bedrooms, 8 baths. Built in 1998.

This is the home of **Richard G. and Leslie West**. Richard is Chairman
and Managing Director of Seattle based Cruise West. The company was
founded by this family in 1973 and specializes in small ship "up close,
casual and personal" cruises. The line started with Alaska cruises and
has expanded to numerous oceans, seas and rivers with nine 52 to 102
passenger ships. This is the largest American-owned cruise line.

Richard is the son of **Chuck West**, nicknamed "Mr. Alaska" for
pioneering Alaskan Tourism. In 1946 Chuck founded Arctic Alaska
Travel Service in Fairbanks and local sightseeing and flight tours over
the Arctic Circle. The company opened the first hotel chain in Alaska.
The Wests moved to Seattle in 1952. The company was renamed
Westours and sold to Holland America Line in 1971.

Mercer Island Information
Luther Burbank Park

(Continued from page 41)
On the east side of **Luther Burbank Park** is the public boat dock, fishing pier, and swimming beach. The park land was homesteaded by **Charles C. Calkins** in 1887. He left this area in 1893. In 1901 a Seattle-based private school for boys bought 10 acres here and built the first building in 1902. The school was called the Parental School and the boys studied and worked on the farm that is now the park. The brick building (right side of above photograph) northwest of the current docks and pier was built in 1929 and was the dormitory for the boys. The school name was changed in 1931 to Luther Burbank School. Washington State took over the school in 1957 and moved the school operations off the island. King County purchased the land in 1969 and the King County Park System developed and maintained the park. In 2003 King County transferred the park to the City of Mercer Island.

Bellevue's Meydenbauer Bay and its Ruby Coast homes are northeast.

Mercer Island Information
Alan Mulally – Boeing, Ford

Alan Mulally, currently President and CEO of **Ford** Motor Company and formerly EVP of **Boeing**, owns a home inland on Mercer Island. He lived here while he was with Boeing. He was with Boeing from 1969, fresh out of college, until 2006. His five children were athletic and academic stars at MIHS. He was hired by Ford in 2006, with a $28 million pay package for his first 4 months, and moved to Michigan but has retained his MI house.

The Boeing Company was founded by **William E. Boeing** in Seattle in 1916. Boeing grew to become the largest aircraft manufacturer in the world following its merger with McDonnell in 1997. Its 2008 revenues were $61 billion. It moved its corporate headquarter to Chicago in 2001 but many divisions and manufacturing facilities have remained in the Puget Sound region.

William E. Boeing came to the Seattle area from Michigan in the early 1900s to go into the lumber business. In 1916 he and a partner founded Pacific Aero Products Co. In 1917 he changed the name to Boeing Airplane Company and received orders for 50 planes from the U.S. Navy as America entered WWI. He lived north of Seattle in the Highlands area overlooking Puget Sound to the west so he personally did not have much to do with development of the south-central Lake Washington waterfront residences. Many of the company's executives have lived on the LW waterfront.

Looking south crossing LW between MI and Bellevue

Mercer Island
Diamond Coast

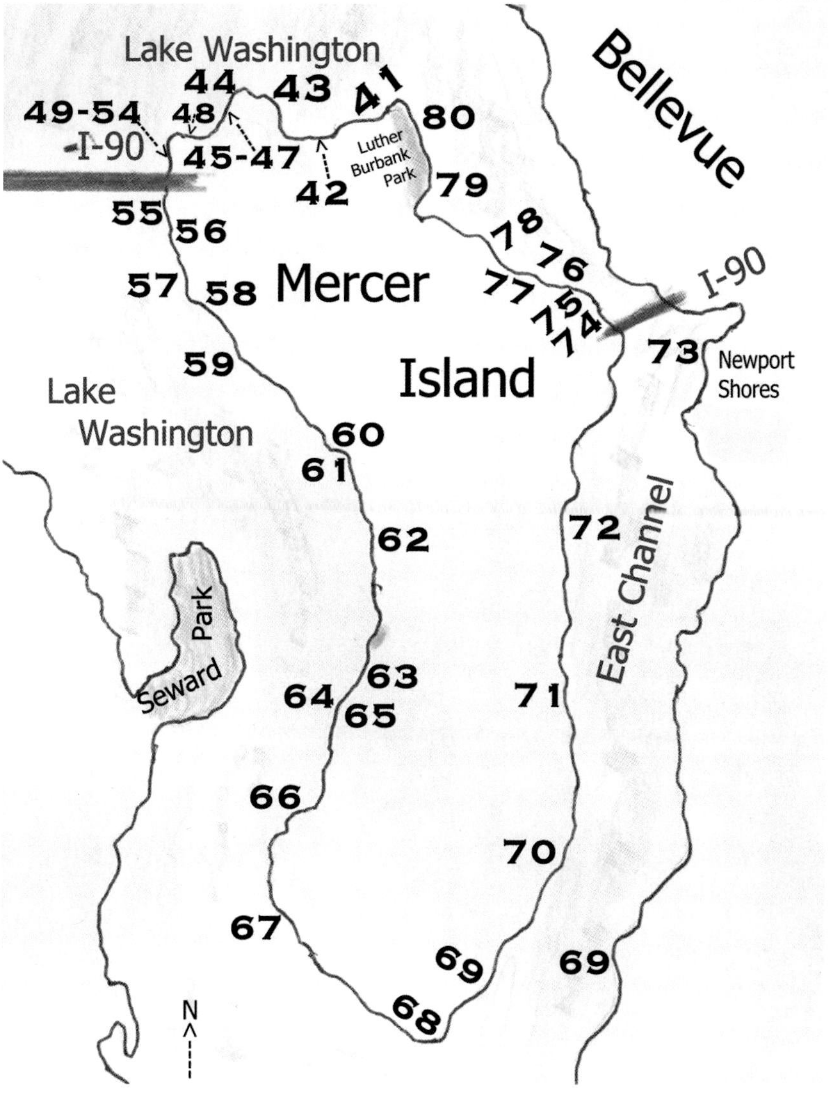

Lake Washington
44
43
41
49-54
48
I-90
45-47
80
Luther Burbank Park
42
79
Bellevue
55
56
78
76
Mercer
57
58
77
75
74
I-90
73
Newport Shores
59
Island
Lake Washington
60
61
62
72
East Channel
Seward Park
63
64
65
71
66
70
67
69
69
68
N

Map not to scale
Numbers refer to page numbers

Bellevue, Medina, Hunts Point and Yarrow Point
Ruby Coast

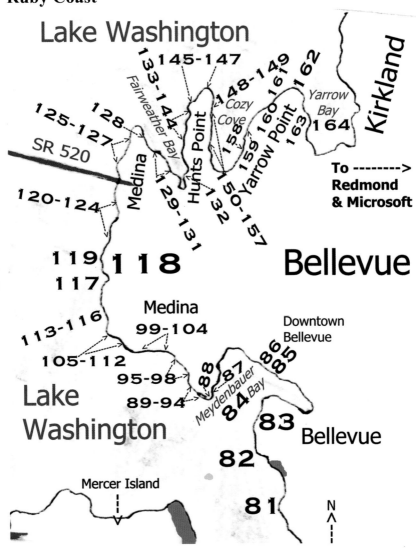

Map not to scale
Numbers refer to page numbers

$9 million Estimated value. 8,160 sq ft on 0.76 acres.
336 feet of waterfront, 5 bedrooms, 8 baths.

The lot and its old house were purchased in 2000 for $5.9 million and this new home was built in 2003. This is our southern-most Bellevue home north of the I-90 East Channel bridge and is northeast of Mercer Island.

This is in the area where Bellevue was settled. This and our estate to the north (next page) are in the Burrows Landing area. The small and first park to the north is **Burrows Landing Park**. The larger park to the immediate north of it is **Chism Park**. **Albert Burrows** was from Des Moines, Iowa and settled here in 1882. The Landing was for the ferry that served this area. Burrows was instrumental in building the original Bellevue schools. He served in the state legislature in 1894 and died in 1896. His son, **Albert Seldon Burrows**, was born in 1871, was in the University of Washington's first graduating class and in 1905 he became King County's superintendent of schools.

Myhrvold, Cameron – Microsoft, Ignition Partners

$9.5 million estimated value. 5,460 sq ft on 2.67 acres.
267 feet of waterfront, 4 bedrooms, 3.75 baths. Built in 1951 and extensively remodeled in 1994. Purchased in 1998 for $5.3 million.

This is the home of **Cameron D. and Linda Myhrvold**. Cameron is a founding partner, along with other former executives of Microsoft and McCaw, of Ignition Partners of Bellevue. Ignition started in 1999 and invests globally in emerging communications, Internet and software businesses and has become one of the largest venture-capital companies in the Northwest. Prior to starting Ignition he was with Microsoft for fourteen years and was Vice President of the Internet Customer Unit. He founded Dynamical Systems, Inc. which he sold to Microsoft in 1986 as he joined the company. The couple is on the honor rolls of many charities. These include PeacePlayers International, Children's Hospital, and the University of Washington. The couple has contributed to Republican candidates.

$11 million estimated value. 10,120 sq ft on 2.1 acres.
183 feet of waterfront, 4 bedrooms, 7.5 baths. Built in 2005.

This is the home of **John J. and Donna Luger**. John and Donna owned Bellevue based Data Base which they sold to Boston based Iron Mountain Inc. in 1999 for $115 million. Iron Mountain is the world's largest records management company. At the time of the sale Data Base was the largest privately owned data-storage company in the nation. The Lugers started Data Base in a Tukwila warehouse in 1976. Following the sale they gave $1 million to establish an endowment at Bellevue's Eastside Catholic High. They are major contributors to the Fulcrum Foundation which supports Catholic schools in the Archdiocese of Seattle. The Lugers' passion is education and they support many private and public schools. The couple has primarily contributed to Republican candidates.

Bellevue Information
Meydenbauer Bay

Meydenbauer Bay is named after Bellevue's first settler-developer, **William Meydenbauer**. Meydenbauer was German born and came to Seattle in the mid 1800s. In 1869 he rowed across Lake Washington, laid claim to 40 acres and built a cabin here. One of the McGilvra family members of Madison Park (page 18) built the first house in this area on Groat Point (page 88) in the 1800s.

"**Bellevue**" is French for "beautiful view." The city was incorporated in 1953 when there were approximately 10,000 residents.

The 2009 population is approximately 120,000 and it is projected to grow to 150,000 by 2050. It is The Eastside's business center and has an estimated daytime population of 180,000. In 2008 *CNNMoney* named Bellevue number 42 in the "Best Places to Live" in the U.S. and number one in the state of Washington. Most of the high rise office and residential buildings in downtown Bellevue were constructed during the past 15 years. Many more are planned.

The city has 5 large high schools and, in 2008, all were ranked in the top 1% of the nation's high schools by *Newsweek* and *U.S. News and World Report*. **Bellevue High** is the public high school for the Ruby Coast cities and towns of Medina, Hunts Point and Yarrow Point plus this Lake Washington shoreline area of Bellevue. In addition to its top academic ratings it is renowned as a sports powerhouse with many championships in multiple sports. Its 21st Century football teams have been nationally ranked and have beaten top California teams. During the 2006-07 basketball season senior **Luke Sikma**, son of **Jack Sikma** (page 86) and sophomore **Alex Schrempf**, son of **Detlef Schrempf** (page 85), played together on a dominating team.

$10 million for sale listing (May 2009). 7,200 sq ft on 0.9 acres. 85 feet of waterfront, 5 bedrooms, 8 baths. This lot with an older home was purchased in 2000 and a new home was built in 2003. The home features covered moorage for a 60 foot yacht, a fabulous great room and kitchen with three fireplaces and a wing for children and guests.

This is the home of **Detlef and Marianne Schrempf**. Detlef starred for the SuperSonics from 1993 to 1999 and was an assistant coach for the team's final 2006-08 seasons in Seattle. He was selected to the NBA All-Star team 3 times and was the first NBA player born in Europe to score 15,000 career points. He was born in West Germany and moved from there to Centralia, Washington in his senior year of high school. He led his school team to the state championship in 1981. He starred at UW and was on the All-PAC-10 Team. He started his NBA career in 1985 being drafted by the Dallas Mavericks. He played on the Sonics team that reached the NBA finals in 1996. He founded the Detlef Schrempf Foundation in 1996 to support organizations that provide hope, care, and assistance to Northwest children and their families. The Foundation hosts the local Detlef Schrempf Celebrity Golf Classic every June.

Bellevue
Zbikowski, Mark – Microsoft
Sikma, Jack – SuperSonics

$8 million for sale listing (May 2009). 7,420 sq ft on 0.69 acres.
85 feet of waterfront, 5 bedrooms, 4.25 baths.

The house was built in 2001 by **Jack and Shawn Sikma** and sold in 2005 to **Mark J. Zbikowski** for $6.7 million. This home features fabulous grounds, carriage house, pool, spa and cabana.

Mark has purchased another house in Yarrow Point. That house and his personal information are on page 159.

Jack is a former star for the Seattle SuperSonics, playing for them from 1977 to 1991 as center. His number 43 jersey was retired by the Sonics in 1992. He led the Sonics to the 1979 NBA championship. He played in seven NBA All-Star Games. He played his final five years for the Milwaukee Bucks. He scored 17,287 points and had 10,816 rebounds during his career. He was noted as one of the most accurate shooting centers with 85% free throw and 33% three point averages. After he retired from playing he was an assistant coach for the Sonics and is now an assistant coach for the Houston Rockets.

$8.5 million estimated value. 7,030 sq ft on 0.61 acres.
145 feet of waterfront, 3 bedrooms, 3.75 baths. Built in 1990.

This is the home of **Frederick H. and Joan Burnstead**. Fred is the owner of Bellevue based Burnstead Construction Co. The Burnstead family represents five generations and more than 50 years of home building in the Northwest. The Burnsteads have three independent and privately held subsidiary companies, The Burnstead Group, Rick Burnstead Construction Co., and Steve Burnstead Construction Co. Fred started The Burnstead Group in 1957 and his sons, Rick and Steve, head up the latter two companies. As of May 2009 they had 19 active communities under development. The couple supports Overlake Hospital and has contributed to Republican candidates.

This is our southeastern-most home in Medina. The Medina-Bellevue border is at the north-west corner of Meydenbauer Bay.

Medina-Bellevue Information
Groat Point

$33.9 million for sale listing (May 2009). 15,160 sq ft on 1.89 acres. 527 feet of waterfront, 5 bedrooms, 9 baths. Built in 1987.

This home features a spectacular 300° view, beautifully landscaped grounds with a large pool, a separate guest house and exquisite workmanship. This is one of the area's fine old estates with outstanding inside and outside areas for large-group entertaining or family quiet time. The current homeowner is a cellular phone pioneer and philanthropist.

This is Groat Point and marks the Medina entrance to Meydenbauer Bay. This has been the site of many famous mansions. The first (**McGilvra**) house was built in the 1800s (page 84). In 1928 **Miller Freeman** purchased and moved into a 14 room mansion on this site. Miller was the owner of a Seattle publishing house and several journals. He was instrumental in getting the Lake Washington Ship Canal built in 1916. He is the father of Kemper Freeman and grandfather of **Kemper Freeman, Jr**. The Kempers have been responsible for major development of Bellevue. Kemper Jr. founded Kemper Development Company which is the major developer of downtown Bellevue.

$8 million estimated value. 7,190 sq ft on 0.6 acres.
155 feet of waterfront, 3 bedrooms, 8 baths. Built in 1995.

This is the home of **J. Lennox Scott**. Lennox is Chairman and CEO of John L. Scott Real Estate. The company was founded in 1931 by his grandfather and has become one of the largest and most successful regional real estate companies in the nation. Lennox is a leader in many trade and community organizations. He is actively involved in the John L. Scott Foundation. The Foundation's primary focus is children's healthcare throughout the Pacific Northwest. He has supported and contributed to Republican candidates.

$8 million estimated value. 7,950 sq ft on 0.65 acres.
118 feet of waterfront, 4 bedrooms, 4.75 baths. Built in 1986.

This is the home of **Richard and Christine DiCerchio**. Richard is Senior Executive Vice President and COO of Issaquah-based Costco. He joined the company in 1983 as VP, Operations. He was appointed Executive VP in 1986, COO – Western Region in 1992, and his current position in 1997. The couple has contributed to Republican candidates.

Costco Wholesale Corporation (the official name) has the largest membership warehouse club chain sales volume in the world with $73 billion sales in 2008. As of May 2009 the company had 555 warehouses, 55 million members in 7 countries and 142,000 employees. The American Customer Satisfaction Index rated Costco number one in the retail industry in 2006. The company also rates high in employee satisfaction. The company's focus is selling quality products at low prices and in high volume. Please see pages 98 and 108 for the founding of Costco.

$9 million estimated value. 7,710 sq ft on 1.17 acres. 157 feet of waterfront, 7 bedrooms, 6.25 baths. Built in 1941 and remodeled in 1994.

This is the home of **Lawrence P. and Mary Hughes**. Lawrence is the owner, Chairman and former CEO of Kent-based American Piledriving Equipment Inc. The company is the world's largest provider of foundation construction equipment. The family has contributed generously to the arts and The University of Washington. The couple has contributed to Republican candidates.

Medina Information
Large lot, old estate

$12 million estimated value. 5,350 sq ft on 1.87 acres.
280 feet of waterfront, 3 bedrooms, 5 baths. Built in 1940.

T. L. Dabney built the first landing in Medina west of here and the point was named Dabney Point (page 101). Ferries went from there to Leschi (page 39) for the Seattleites to get to this area which they called "Points Country." The local community selected "Medeena," after the Arabian city, as the name. The name evolved to "Medina." Estates were established in this area.

This is the view looking south. The I-90 East Channel bridge is in the lower right. **Scott Oki**'s (page 145) flagship golf course club Newcastle, is on top of the relatively bare hill in the upper left with fantastic views of the lake, sound and Seattle and Bellevue skylines.

92

$9 million estimated value. 10,250 sq ft on 0.96 acres.
120 feet of waterfront, 10 bedrooms, 6.5 baths. Built in 1947.

This is the home of **Charles M. and Yvonne Pigott.** Charles was President and CEO of Bellevue-based PACCAR, Inc. He led the company from 1965 to when he retired in 1996. Charles is on Harvard Business School's List of 20th Century American Leaders for his leadership in taking Pacific Car and Foundry from a small family company to an industry leader. It changed its name to PACCAR in 1972. PACCAR is recognized as the truck manufacturing world leader and has numerous manufacturing facilities in the greater Seattle area. Kenworth, Peterbilt and DAF are its vehicles' nameplates. The company was founded by Charles' grandfather, William Pigott, Sr., in 1905. After a change in ownership, Paul Pigott, Charles' father, acquired a major interest in the company in 1934. Charles' son, Mark Pigott (page 113), became Chairman and CEO in 1997. Charles served on the board of directors of Boeing and *The Seattle Times* and as president of the Boy Scouts of America. The couple is a major contributor to the Fulcrum Foundation which supports Catholic schools in the Archdiocese of Seattle. The couple has contributed to Republican candidates.

Simonyi, Charles – Microsoft, Astronaut

$25 million estimated value. 19,040 sq ft on 1.32 acres.
302 feet of waterfront, 4 bedrooms, 6.5 baths. Built in 1989 and renovated in 1995. There is an additional picture on page 4.

This is the home of Hungarian-born **Charles Simonyi**. The home is known locally as the "**Windows 2000 House**" and "**Villa Simonyi**," It was designed for Charles when he was with Microsoft. He acquired 3 lots on which to build. The main house is designed to connect free flowing space with inside living. The round master bed automatically rotates with the sun to capture sunlight and the changing views. The home features angled walls, windows and mirrors to maximize the views and provide natural lighting for an exquisite art collection, a unique 60-foot lap pool and a workout room. When Microsoft introduced Windows 2000 a few windows were added to the house to bring the total to 2,000.

Charles joined Microsoft in 1981 at the age of 33 and oversaw the development of Excel and Word. He was previously with Xerox. He left Microsoft in 2002 and co-founded Bellevue-based Intentional Software where he is President. The company develops and markets unique software development tools. He was one of the initial commercial astronauts. He paid $25 million for a 2007 two-week International Space Station roundtrip aboard the Russian Soyuz space shuttles. He paid $35 million for a similar trip in 2009. He has established the Charles Simonyi Fund for Arts and Sciences. The Fund has granted millions of dollars to area educational, science and arts organizations and has endowed chairs at Oxford University and Stanford University. He has contributed to Republican candidates.

$15 million estimated value. 12,250 sq ft on 1.31 acres.
175 feet of waterfront, 7 bedrooms, 7.25 baths.   Built in 1989.
Purchased in 1999 for $13 million.

The estate is known as Diamanti – Greek for diamond. The house has a pool within a two-story glass atrium, a professional recording studio, garages for 10 cars and rooms for exercise, saunas and spas. The auto museum garage is connected to the house with a glass wall for viewing.

This is the home of **Naveen Jain**. Naveen joined Microsoft in 1989 as a senior executive. He left the company in 1996 to found Bellevue-based InfoSpace, Inc., a provider of Internet services. He left that company in 2002 amidst lawsuits but stayed on the board of directors until 2005. In 2003 he founded Bellevue-based Intelius, specializing in Internet searches of public records. He is the CEO of the company. He was listed by *Forbes* in 2000 as one of the wealthiest people in the world with a net worth estimated at $2.2 billion before InfoSpace stock fell from $1,000 per share to $3.90 in 2002. Please see page 56 for another house *The Seattle Times* reported Naveen owns. He has contributed to both major parties.

$7.9 million for sale listing (May 2009). 6,200 sq ft on 0.64 acres.
42 feet of waterfront, 5 bedrooms, 4 baths. Built in 1959.

From the Internet listing: "With a nod to traditionalism ~ past the coach house, the terra cotta courtyard and to the spectacular pool and wade-in lakefront. Just a 5% grade. The dynamic touch of master R. David Adams so evident. French doors; orangey; shutters, shadow boxes and knot gardens. Brick hearth and bay window in the country kitchen. Crown moldings; breadboard. Stepping softly to a world of yesterday; nestled among the giants while holding a stature of its own. Upscale Gold Coast waterfront. Softly, yesterday!"

$30 million estimated value. 19,570 sq ft on 2.04 acres.
115 feet of waterfront, 4 bedrooms, 9.5 baths. Built in 2000.

This is the home of **Nathan P. Myhrvold**. Along with Edward Jung, he co-founded Bellevue-based Intellectual Ventures in 2000. Both were previously top scientists at Microsoft. Intellectual Ventures invests in invention. The company has created and purchased thousands of patents and original inventions with the purpose of protecting the inventors and collecting royalties from larger companies. Nathan personally holds 18 U.S. patents and has applications pending for 100 more. He was born in Seattle, earned a PhD in theoretical and mathematical physics from Princeton at the age of 23 in 1981. He joined a computer startup company, Dynamical Systems, Inc., and became CEO. The company was purchased by Microsoft in 1986 and he joined Microsoft as Chief Technology Officer. He founded Microsoft Research in 1991. He is a prize winning nature and wildlife photographer and a master French chef, occasionally working as an assistant chef at a restaurant. He has contributed more than $1 million to scientific foundations. He has contributed to Democratic candidates.

$24 million estimated value. 11,500 sq ft on 2.35 acres.
215 feet of waterfront, 3 bedrooms, 5 baths. Built in 2003.

This is the home of **Jeffrey H. and Susan Brotman**. Jeffrey is the Chairman and co-founder, with **James Sinegal** (page 108 and 144), of Costco. Jeffrey and Susan both grew up in the retailing business. Jeffrey was born in Tacoma in 1942 and his father, Bernie, operated 18 retail clothing stores in the 1970s. Susan was born in 1949 in Hamilton, Montana and was a buyer for Nordstrom's in Seattle when she met Jeffrey in 1975 on a blind date at a Sonics game. They married the following year. Jeffrey received a law degree from UW in 1967, briefly practiced law, returned to retailing and from the mid 1980s to mid 1990s, with brother Michael, opened and operated the Jeffrey Michael chain of men's stores. Jeffrey was intrigued with Price Club in California and contacted Sinegal. See page 108 for the rest of the founding story and page 90 for more Costco information.

The couple has generously supported many causes including education, health care, the arts, diversity and Jewish organizations. UW and the Seattle Art Museum have been $10 million plus recipients. The couple was named "First Citizens of 2005" by the Seattle-King County Association of Realtors. Jeffrey is a Regent for UW and is on the Board of Directors of Starbucks. The couple has contributed to Democratic candidates.

$10 million estimated value. 5,330 sq ft on 2.59 acres.
150 feet of waterfront, 5 bedrooms, 4.75 baths. Built in 1929.

This is the home of **Diana Neely**. Her late husband, **Michael G. Neely**, died in 1995 of cancer. Michael was a prominent attorney with the Helsell Paul firm in Seattle. He was also with Washington Arbitration and Mediation Service Inc. He was a recognized mediator. Diana supports The University of Washington Cancer Center and other charities. She has contributed to Republican candidates.

Reed, William – Simpson Investment

$20 million estimated value. 8,610 sq ft on 5.36 acres.
305 feet of waterfront, 7 bedrooms, 4.5 baths.

Built in 1928 and remodeled in 2002. The estate features fabulously landscaped grounds with a tennis court (front left of upper picture). This and the estate on page 112 have the largest waterfront parcels in Medina.

This is the home of **William G. Jr. and Victoria Reed**. He is or has been on the Boards of Microsoft, Paccar, Safeco, The Seattle Times Company and Washington Mutual. The couple is noted as major donors directly and through Simpson Investment to numerous local charities and the arts. The couple has contributed to Republican candidates.

(Continued from page 22) William is part of the Reed dynasty that has led Tacoma-based Simpson Investment Company. He is the son **William G. Reed Sr**. who ran the company from 1942 to 1971 and continued the company's diversification. William Jr. worked in executive positions starting in the 1960s and served as Chairman from 1971 to 1996. He oversaw the company's expansion into plastics and other manufacturing. His nephew, **Colin Moseley**, has been Chairman since 1996. Colin's father, **Furman Moseley**, brother-in-law of William Jr., was a president of Simpson and lives on the old Reed estate in Madison Park (page 22).

100

$9 million estimated value. 9,600 sq ft on 0.65 acres.
105 feet of waterfront, 5 bedrooms, 5.75 baths. Built in 2002.

This is the home of **Lars H. and Laurie McDonald Jonsson**. Lars is the CEO and founder (1989) of Seattle-based Stellar One Corporation, a family-owned real estate firm with a diverse global portfolio in Sweden, Poland and the Pacific Northwest. Laurie is on the Board. She, and her brother and father (McDonalds) were involved with the start of the company (see page 138). Lars came to the United States in 1986 from Sweden where he held CEO and other executive positions with Swedish companies. Laurie was featured in a 1997 *Seattle Times* article. The article said she had "built, run and sold a cruise ship company, made a bundle in real estate and launched a luxury travel service." The article reported that she was the number one Democratic political contributor in the state in 1996 with a $141,000 contribution and that she was involved in major fund raisers locally and in Washington, D.C. attended by the President and VP. She is the daughter of **Stanley McDonald**, the founder of Princess Cruises, and the sister of **Kirby McDonald** (page 138). The couple has been a major contributor to Democratic candidates.

This is **Dabney Point** (information on page 92).

$15 million estimated value. 13,040 sq ft on 1.92 acres.
198 feet of waterfront, 4 bedrooms, 5.5 baths. Built in 1997.

This is the home of **Gary and Michela MacLeod**. Gary was Chairman of Bellevue-based Magnadrive Corporation from 1999 to 2008. The company was founded in 1999 and manufactures patented specialty torque management devices. He is Chairman Emeritus of Seattle-based Laird Norton Trust Company where he was Chairman and CEO from 1975 to 1999. This is a private trust and management company and is known for its philanthropy.

$10 million estimated value. 12,270 sq ft on 0.86 acres.
110 feet of waterfront, 7 bedrooms, 7.5 baths. Built in 1991.

This is the home of **Dr. Howard and Mary Maron**. Howard is recognized as the founder of "concierge medicine." He co-founded, with Dr. I. Scott Hall, Bellevue-based MD^2 in 1996. The firm's statement is "the definitive provider of concierge medicine. . . unlimited access to your personal physician. . . 24/7 care – in your home . . . only 50 families per doctor . . . " He is former physician for the Seattle SuperSonics. The couple supports many local charities and is a large supporter of America Scores, a community youth-development organization. The couple has contributed to Republican candidates.

Medina Information

Medina City Hall and Beach Park

The City of Medina is a low-density residential community with a population of 3,500. It has 4.5 miles of waterfront and 1.6 square miles of land. The city ranks number 2 behind Hunts Point in the state in per capita income with $82,000. The waterfront boundaries are with Bellevue to the east in Meydenbauer Bay and with Hunts Point to the north around Evergreen Point in Fairweather Bay.

Miller Freeman (page 88) was one of the early community leaders in the early 1900s and was instrumental in establishing the early schools. In the early 1900s the area was primarily farms. **Overlake Country Club** was built inland in 1920 just up the hill from here and within what is now the city limits. It was and still is a highly rated golf course and club. It was originally a popular week-end retreat for Seattleites and is now the country club for residents of Medina and the surrounding Eastside communities.

The city was incorporated in 1955. It remained a sleepy community until the development of downtown Bellevue and Microsoft in Redmond began in the 1980s. This waterfront became very popular and values skyrocketed. Medina has two public elementary schools and the city is in the Bellevue school district.

Please see page 141 city's and the other Points Communities' statistical data. Per capita incomes are on page 144.

Jeff Bezos lives on one of the largest waterfront estates, five acres, in Medina. He founded Seattle-based **Amazon.Com** in 1994 and is its President, CEO and COB. The company is the pioneer of large-scale Internet retail sales. *Time* magazine named Jeff the 1999 "Person of the Year." In 2003 and 2004 *Forbes* listed him as number one in its list of top performing CEOs in America.

Jeff grew up in the Southwest and South, graduated from Princeton in the mid 1980s and went to work on Wall Street. He became intrigued with the growing Internet and the high-tech explosion in the Seattle area. In 1993 he drove to Seattle from NY, wrote his business plan in the car and set up business in a Seattle garage. In 1995 Amazon started selling books on-line. Jeff named the company after the world's largest river. The company now sells a wide range of products. It is the largest on-line retailer with an annual sales rate of more the $25 billion.

In 1997 Amazon went public with its stock at $18 per share ($1.50 adjusted for splits). The stock split in 1998 and twice in 1999. Adjusted for these splits, the peak stock price was $107 in 1999 and its next low was $7 in 2001. Please see page 68 for 2006-2009 sales and stock information. Amazon's headquarters building can be seen from LW; it is a large old brick building on the top of Seattle's Beacon Hill less than a mile west of the I-90 Bridge.

Jeff purchased a $30 million estate in Beverly Hills in early 2007 which was splashed over the Internet. He has been listed by *Forbes* as one of the wealthiest people in the world with his 2008 net worth estimated at $8.7 billion. He has contributed primarily to Democratic candidates.

View from Medina with sunset over Madison Park

105

McCaw, Bruce – McCaw Cellular
McCaw, John – McCaw Cellular

Bruce McCaw lives on a prominent waterfront estate in Medina. Please see page 152 for the McCaw family story. Bruce is the oldest of four brothers (below and pages 38 and 153) who were the pioneers of cellular communications. He had been listed by *Forbes* as one of the wealthiest people in the world but has not been on its recent lists as a result of declining stock market values. He is now involved in large scale commercial real estate investments with his Pistol Creek Financial Co. He is also involved in auto racing as president of Bellevue-based PacWest Racing Group LLC and director of Michigan-based Championship Auto Racing Teams, Inc. Bruce and his wife, Jolene, are major contributors to Seattle-based Talaris Institute and are co-chairs of its board. Charity organization Talaris focuses on early childhood development. They are prominent benefactors for education, the arts and other organizations. He has contributed primarily to Republican candidates.

John McCaw, Jr. is the third born of the four brothers. He was Executive VP for McCaw cellular. He owns property in Seattle and numerous other areas along with a large luxury yacht. He has been a part-owner of the Vancouver Canucks NHL franchise and the Seattle Mariners where he was also a member of the Board. He had also been listed by *Forbes* as one of the wealthiest people in the world but has not been on its recent lists.

A Yacht on Lake Washington

$9.5 million estimated value. 9,450 sq ft on 0.7 acres.
92 feet of waterfront, 5 bedrooms, 5.25 baths. Built in 1990. Purchased in 1999 for $6.9 million and renovated in 2000.

This is the home of **Wayne M. & Christine Perry**. Wayne is International Commissioner of the Boy Scouts of America and former President of McCaw Cellular. He has law degrees from Northwestern and NY Universities. Starting in 1976, Wayne provided legal counsel to McCaw Cellular Communications (page 152). In 1981 Wayne and Dick Monroe founded Seattle-based Monroe & Perry law firm which evolved into the prominent Stokes Lawrence firm. He served McCaw in executive positions while starting the new law firm. He left the law firm and became President of McCaw in 1985. He served as Vice-Chairman of AT&T Wireless after McCaw merged with them in 1994. He was a Cub Scout as a young boy and has been involved with the Boy Scouts of America ever since. Previous positions include president of the Chief Seattle Council and president of the Western Region. He was named International Commissioner in 2006. The couple has contributed to Republican candidates.

$7.5 million estimated value. 6,200 sq ft on 0.8 acres.
95 feet of waterfront, 4 bedrooms, 5 baths. Built in 1998.

This is the home of **James D. and Janet Sinegal**. The couple owns a larger house in Hunts Point (page 144). James is the President, CEO and co-founder, with Jeffrey Brotman (page 98), of Costco. The couple has generously contributed to numerous charities with an emphasis on education at all levels. James is on the Board of Trustees of Seattle University. The couple has contributed to Democratic candidates and has been very active in numerous Democratic political campaigns and local ballot initiatives.

James and **Jeffrey Brotman** (page 98) founded Costco in Kirkland in 1983 and opened its first warehouse in Seattle. Costco was the first company in U.S. history to grow from zero to $3 billion in annual sales in less than 6 years. James started his retail career in 1954 as a bagger for FedMart. He worked with Sol and Robert Price in San Diego to form Price Club in 1976. Price Club's first San Diego warehouse was an old Howard Hughes airplane hanger. In 1993 Costco and Price Club were similar in size with about $8 billion each in annual sales and the two companies merged. The combined company was initially run by executives from both of the prior companies but the Price brothers left in 1994 and Price Club stores became Costcos. *Business Week* named James one of the "Best Managers" of 2003 and *Time Magazine* put him on its 2006 list of "The 100 Most Influential People." See page 98 for more of the founding story and page 90 for more Costco information.

$9.5 million estimated value. 9,775 sq ft on 0.89 acres.
102 feet of waterfront, 5 bedrooms, 5 baths. Built in 2000.

This is the home of **Charles G. and Delphine Stevens**. Charles is the former Microsoft Corporate Enterprise Sales Vice President. He joined the company in 1984 and retired in 2008. During his career with the company he held worldwide marketing, sales and development positions. He was born in Great Britain, received an MBA from Harvard, became a U.S. citizen and was a product manger for Hewlett-Packard prior to joining Microsoft. He is now on the Board of Directors of California-based Applied Voice and Speech Technologies, Inc. Charles has contributed to the Microsoft PAC which supports both major parties.

$15 million estimated value. 14,030 sq ft on 1.96 acres.
175 feet of waterfront, 4 bedrooms, 5 baths.

This is the home of **Gerald B. and Carolyn Grinstein. Jack and Shawn Sikma** of the Sonics (page 86) lived here in a previous house. They sold that house and property in 1993 for $8 million to the Grinsteins who built this house in 2000.

Gerald is the former CEO of Atlanta-based Delta Air Lines, Inc. He was born in Seattle. He was a partner in the Seattle-based Preston Gates law firm from 1969 to 1983. In 1984 he became CEO of Los Angeles-based Western Airlines and it and Delta merged in 1987. Following the merger he was on Delta's Board of Directors while becoming President and CEO of Burlington Northern Railroad from 1989 to 1995. In 2004, amid Delta's financial problems and controversy over executive compensation and perks, he was appointed CEO. He oversaw major restructuring of the company. It successfully emerged from bankruptcy in early 2007 and he retired later in the year. He served as administrative assistant to the late U.S. Senator **Warren Magnuson**. He is on PACCAR's Board of Directors. The couple has contributed generously to the area's arts and education. Gerald is a past president of the UW Board of Regents. He graduated from UW where his father served as the football teams' physician. The couple has contributed to Democratic candidates.

La Haye, Peter (1940-1999) – Eye Lenses Inventor

$45 million listed for sale in 1999. 24,130 sq ft on 5.12 acres. 372 feet of waterfront, 6 bedrooms, 9 baths. Built in 1992. The home includes 14 fireplaces and a hydraulic system for revolving bookcases that open into secret rooms.

This is the home of **Sandra La Haye**. Her husband **Peter** died in 1999 in a Pennsylvania crash of a private jet. Peter dropped out of high school and joined the Marines. In 1959 he went to work in the optical division of Bell & Howell in Los Angeles. He also started inventing in his garage and in 1973 he was on his own developing lenses for implants in cataract patients. He formed his own company, Iolab. By 1980 his company controlled over 50% of the market for these lenses and he sold the company to Johnson & Johnson for an estimated $80 million and he and Sandra moved to Washington State. They bought this lot and its previous house in 1986 for $2.6 million. The new house took six years to build and was completed in 1992. Peter started two Redmond-based companies, La Haye Laboratories and Neoptx, in the mid 1990s. The companies were involved with lenses and supplements for eye diseases. The couple has contributed to and been involved with numerous charities with an emphasis on reducing diseases in developing countries. Peter was flying to a board meeting of Orbis International, a charity that promotes eye health in developing nations, when his plane crashed.

Medina Estate

$35 million estimated value. 13,160 sq ft in two separate houses on 5.34 acres. 310 feet of waterfront, 9 bedrooms, 8 baths. The first house (8,300 sq ft) was built in 1940 and renovated in 2000. The second house (4,860 sq ft) was built in 2004.

This and the estate on page 100 have the largest waterfront parcels in Medina. This lot and the one on the previous page stretch over 200 yards from the shoreline to Evergreen Point Road.

The estate was purchased in 1998 for $10 million by an Internet pioneer as Internet commerce exploded. The existing house was extensively modernized and construction of a second house was completed in 2004. Because the lot is very large and wooded it is hard to see much of these structures from the water. A $28 million permit was obtained in 2008 for new construction. The large boat-dock/house, approximately 6,000 sq ft, was recently rebuilt and can house in privacy some of the owner's yachts. It can also be used for lakeside parties. Under the state's **Shoreline Management Act** covering Lake Washington, building new docks is very restrictive. An existing dock and its footprint are grandfathered as long as the dock is maintained within the act's standards. Boat houses cannot be built but an existing one can be rebuilt on its footprint. The square footage of boat houses (and garages) is not included in a parcel's (living) square footage.

$7.5 million estimated value. 6,080 sq ft on 1.48 acres.
106 feet of waterfront, 4 bedrooms, 3.25 baths. Built in 1987.

This is the home of **Mark and Cindy Pigott**. Mark is the Chairman and CEO of Bellevue-based PACCAR, Inc. (page 93). He is the fourth generation of the Pigott family to lead the company. He started with the company in 1978 and assumed his current top position in 1997. Under his leadership the company has continued to prosper financially and with many industry, quality and customer satisfaction awards. In 2004 *Forbes* listed him number five in its list of top performing CEOs in America. The couple is very active in local philanthropy. Mark is President of the PACCAR Foundation. The foundation supports education, social services and the arts with annual donations of more than $10 million. In 2008 the UW Michael G. Foster School of Business named a new building "PACCAR Hall" in recognition of an $18 million gift from PACCAR and the Pigott family. UW receives an annual $35,000 honorarium to award to a professor the PACCAR Award for Teaching Excellence. Mark has contributed to Republican candidates.

113

$9 million estimated value. 7,200 sq ft on 1.47 acres.
188 feet of waterfront, 5 bedrooms, 5.25 baths. Built in 2000.
Purchased in 2005 for $6.9 million and extensively remodeled.

This is the home of **Douglas E. and Charlotte Guyman**. Both are
retired Microsoft executives.   Charlotte has been on the Board of
Directors of Warren Buffet's Berkshire Hathaway since 2003. She had
been Microsoft's GM of MSN Internet sales, Director of International
Marketing, and Director of Consumer Division Marketing. She is a
close friend of Melinda Gates (page 118) and the two have traveled
together overseas to poor countries viewing the needs for the Gates
Foundation's grants for reducing AIDS and other diseases in these
countries. Charlotte is Vice Chairman of the BOD of UW Medicine.

The home to the south (right in picture at the top) is a landmark for its
replica **Statue of Liberty**. A former owner from New York felt this area
should have its welcome and liberty symbol for newcomers.

$9 million estimated value. 5,560 sq ft on 3.14 acres.
140 feet of waterfront, 5 bedrooms, 4 baths. Built in 1918. This is one of the fine old Medina homes on a large lot that stretches over 200 yards from the shoreline to Evergreen Point Road.

This is the home of **Hugh S. Ferguson**. Hugh founded Seattle-based Ferguson Construction in 1948. Under his leadership the company expanded in commercial construction throughout the entire West Coast and into the Southwest. Notable projects include the building of Costco and Home Depot warehouses/stores. He is retired and Chairman Emeritus. He is now known for his philanthropy through the Hugh and Jane (1918-1994) Ferguson Foundation. His wife, Jane, died in 1994, and he and their daughter, Ellen Ferguson, funded a room in the foundation's name in the new Seattle Library. The foundation has been involved in numerous community charities and causes.

$7.8 million for sale listing (May 2009). 6,320 sq ft on 0.73 acres. 115 feet of waterfront, 5 bedrooms, 5.5 baths. Built in 2007.

From the Internet listing: "A Tuscan treasure sited at the 50 yard view line focused on spectacular cityscapes of towers and neonic hues, snowcapped Olympic peaks, full breadth of Lake Washington. 115' of superb level shore lands; new dock being installed. An interior arcade of satin smooth Doric columns, Roman arches heeding a sense of scale and light. Incorporating the framework for a home that should be lived in; terrific indoor play spaces; a fresh air pool pavilion and fireplace at waters edge. The genius of privacy."

$9 million estimated value. 6,950 sq ft on 0.49 acres. 160 feet of waterfront, 4 bedrooms, 5.25 baths. Built in 2003.

This is the home of **Bob and Jan Whitsitt**. Bob is former General Manger of the SuperSonics and the Seahawks. Bob and Jan now run home-based Whitsitt Enterprises, LLC. The firm provides consulting, negotiating, business development, marketing, media relations and sports franchise management services. Bob started his professional sports management career at the age of 22 in 1978 as an intern with the NBA Indiana Pacers. In 1982 he was a VP with the NBA Kansas City Kings and was a key player in the teams' move to Sacramento. Jan had been with ABC Sports in New York and then was with Seattle's KOMO-TV when she met Bob at a league meeting. They were married in 1986 and before she could move to Sacramento, **Barry Ackerley** (page 33) hired Bob as President (the NBA's youngest at 30) and General Manager of the Seattle SuperSonics. He was named the 1994 NBA Executive of the Year. He was hailed as the architect of the 1995-96 Sonics NBA finals team although he had a falling-out with Ackerley. In 1994 he took the GM job with the NBA Portland Trailblazers owned by **Paul Allen** (page 64). In 1997 Allen gave him a second job as President of Allen's NFL Seattle Seahawks. Bob left the Trailblazers in 2000 and left the Seahawks after the 2004-2005 season following a power struggle with **Mike Holmgren** (page 67). Jan had a stint as VP of marketing and broadcasting for the Sonics.

Gates, Bill and Melinda – Microsoft

$150 million estimated value. 50,050 sq ft on 5.15 acres.
475 feet of waterfront, 8 bedrooms, 25 baths. Built from 1994 to 1996.

This is the home of **Bill and Melinda Gates** and the most famous waterfront estate on Lake Washington. Bill co-founded Microsoft (page 12), with **Paul Allen** (page 64), and is Chairman. He stepped down as CEO in 2000. Bill and Melinda are Co-Chairs of the Bill & Melinda Gates Foundation. For many years, Bill has been listed by Forbes as the wealthiest person in the world with his estimated 2008 net worth $57 billion.

Melinda received an MBA from Duke in 1987 and went to work for Microsoft in Redmond as a product marketing manager. She met Bill the same year at a Microsoft press event in New York. She continued with Microsoft and was highly regarded as a top performer. She rose to GM of information products. They married in 1994 and co-founded the foundation the same year. She is considered the driving force of the foundation which has given charities over $20 billion. In 2008 *Forbes* ranked her number 40 on their list of the 100 Most Powerful Women. They have three children, Jennifer Katharine (1996), Rory John (1999) and Phoebe Adele (2002). The couple has contributed to the Microsoft PAC which supports both major parties. (Continued on next page)

(Continued from previous page)   The buildings took four years to construct at an estimated cost of about $100 million.   Timbers aged about 500 years were obtained from an ancient lumber mill.   There is an elevator or 84 steps from the grand entrance down to the ground floor. The family's inner sanctum is about 11,500 square feet.   Other areas include a reception hall plus multiple conference and dining rooms for 200-plus people.   There is a state-of-the-art theater.   The 17 by 60 foot indoor/outdoor pool has an underwater music system.   The main library houses Leonardo da Vinci's original Codex Leicester that Bill purchased in 1994 for $30.8 million.   It is exhibited for a brief period at a different location in the world each year.

The house features the ultimate in computerized electronics for entertainment, lighting, climate control and security.   Guests receive a computerized pin when they arrive.   Each pin is coded to emit an individualized signal that permits access to specific rooms and keeps track of each guest.   Your previously selected TV show, movie or art with music on HDTV, climate and lighting will follow you from room to room.   If you receive a phone call, only the phone nearest you will ring.

A wetland estuary with streams was created for an environmentally favorable utilization of runoff.   It is stalked with salmon, sea-run cutthroat trout and exotic species.

Shirley, Jon – Microsoft

Shirley top center – Gates bottom right

$40 million estimated value. 27,255 sq ft on 4.35 acres.
244 feet of waterfront, 2 bedrooms, 6 baths. Built in 2000.

If you are cruising north see page 124 for more description of this
section of Medina. Construction of this mansion, known as the Orchard
Project, began in 1998.

This is the home of **Jon and Mary Shirley**. Jon was President and COO
of Microsoft from 1983 to 1990 when he retired. He remains as a
director of the company and is also a director of Seattle-based Manzanita
Capital, a financial services company. The couple is a major donor to
and supporter of local charities and the arts. Jon is Chairman of the
Board of Trustees of the Seattle Art Museum and on the Chairman's
Council of New York City's Museum of Modern Art. The couple
collects art and vintage racing Ferraris. The couple has contributed to
Democratic candidates.

Foster center   -   Shirley right

$10 million estimated value. 10,710 sq ft on 1.45 acres. 124 feet of waterfront, 6 bedrooms, 6.25 baths. Built in 2007. The lot with an old house was purchased in 2005 for $4.4 million.

This is the home of **Michael Greg Foster, Jr.** He and Jill Goodsell run Seattle-based The Foster Foundation. Jill is Executive Director and he is Trustee. UW's **Michael G. Foster School of Business** is named after his father who passed away in 2003. The UW Business School was given its current name by the Board of Regents in 2007 following a $36.5 million gift by the foundation. That gift brought the foundation's total contributions to the school to $50 million. The Foster family has a strong legacy of PNW philanthropy contributing to education, the arts, health, children and homeless programs. The foundation was established in 1984 by **Michael Sr.**, his father, **Albert O. Foster**, and Albert's wife, **Evelyn**. Albert founded Foster & Marshall, Seattle's first firm to own a seat on the NY Stock Exchange. Michael Sr. was president of the firm from 1971 to 1982 when it was bought by Shearson/American Express for $76 million.

Gaudette, Francis J. (1936-1993) – Microsoft

$10 million estimated value. 10,000 sq ft on 2.46 acres.
129 of feet waterfront, 5 bedrooms, 10.25 baths. Built in 1992.

This is the home of **Doris H. Gaudette**. Doris was the wife of **Francis J. Gaudette** who was Executive Vice President and CFO at Microsoft. He joined the company in 1984 and was instrumental in organizing the company's initial public stock offering in 1986. He died of cancer at the age of 57 in 1993. The couple was generous in their support of charities and the arts, especially local performing arts theaters. The **Francis J. Gaudette Theater in Issaquah** was built in 1994 and named in his honor. Doris has continued the legacy of philanthropy.

$9 million estimated value. 7,780 sq ft on 1.71 acres.
172 feet of waterfront which extends in front of the large house to the north which has no waterfront. 5 bedrooms, 7 baths. Built in 1995.

In this area of Medina the bluff is over 100 feet above the water. Many of the bluff houses are hard to see from the water because they are high on the hill offering fantastic views! Because of the height, many estates have trams. The stairways from the bluff to water level have over 200 stairs.

Medina Bluff Area

$12 million estimated value. 13,200 sq ft on 2.37 acres.
147 feet of waterfront, 5 bedrooms, 6.25 baths. Built in 1967.

This is our northern-most Medina home south of the SR-520 bridge. The large mansion on this large estate is hard to see from the water because of the trees on the bank. The mega-lots (lots over two acres) in this section, from page 120 to here, of Medina stretch over 200 yards from the shoreline to Evergreen Point Road.

A private investment and conservationist couple live here. They have contributed to Democratic candidates.

124

$7.9 million for sale listing (May 2009). 8,030 sq ft on 0.63 acres.
71 feet of waterfront, 5 bedrooms, 7.5 baths. Built in 2003.

From the Internet listing: "Resort Living on Medina's Gold Coast. Unparalleled specifications, exquisite Vasos Demetriou designed, Bender Chaffey built contemporary home. Seamless integration of soothing indoor/outdoor pool and spa. Olympic mountain, Seattle skyline and lake views, elegant gardens, urban dynamics and the local wildlife. Five top floor bedrooms, eight total baths. Remarkable finishes of striking beauty. Luxurious amenities affording effortless comfort to those who know and appreciate the best."

This is the home of **Pieter C. and Anne Knook**. Pieter was with Microsoft as Senior Vice President of the Mobile Communications Business and left the company in March to join UK-based mobile operator Vodafone Group PLC as Director of Internet Services.

This is our southwestern-most Medina home north of the 520 bridge, formally named The Evergreen Point Floating Bridge.

$15 million 7/16/2006 purchase price. 7,050 sq ft on 1.15 acres.
176 feet of waterfront, 4 bedrooms, 5 baths. Built in 1998.

This is the home of **Michael R. and Linda Mastro**. Michael is the founder and owner of Mastro Properties. The company was founded in 1966 and has developed and sold over $1 billion of subdivision infrastructures, office buildings, high-tech facilities, residential condominiums and retirement communities in the greater Puget Sound region. The couple supports numerous local charities, the University of Washington and the arts. The couple has contributed to Republican candidates.

This peninsula of Medina is **Evergreen Point**. Fairweather Bay is on the other side of the point.

$8.8 million for sale listing (May 2009). 7,365 sq ft on 0.63 acres. 134 feet of waterfront, 5 bedrooms, 5 baths. Built in 1987. Purchased in 2005 for $7 million. This home features a prime view, lush landscaping with a brook and pond, a large game room with a second kitchen, and two docks.

This is the home of **Christopher P. and Patricia Liddell**. Christopher has been with Microsoft as Senior Vice President and CFO since 2005. He came to Microsoft from International Paper where he was Sr. VP & CFO. He was born in New Zealand.

May, Peter – University of Washington

$8 million estimated value. 4,970 sq ft on .7 acres.
119 feet of waterfront, 5 bedrooms, 4.75 baths.

Built in 1927 and updated in 1996. Purchased in 2006 for $7 million.
This is one of the beautiful original homes in this area that has been
updated preserving the original look and charm. Most of this area's
original homes have been demolished for newer ones.

This is the home of **Peter J. and Patricia May**. Peter is a Professor,
Political Science, at UW in the Center for American Politics and Public
Policy. He has published numerous papers and has received teaching
and research awards.

This is our northeastern-most home in Fairweather Bay on Medina's
Evergreen Point peninsula.

$12.5 million price purchased 3/31/2008 from John F. Buchan Construction, Inc. who purchased it in 2007 for $14 million.
6,610 sq ft on 0.96 acres.
113 feet of waterfront, 4 bedrooms, 4.75 baths. Built in 1998.

We are in **Fairweather Bay** with Medina to the west and Hunts Point to the east. Residents like the protected waters of this bay and Cozy Cove on the other side of Hunts Point.

Fairweather Bay – Medina – Microsoft

$9 million estimated value. 9,330 sq ft on 1.84 acres.
78 feet of waterfront, 5 bedrooms, 7 baths. Built in 2001.

This is the home of a couple who both work for Microsoft. They have
contributed to Republican candidates.

$9.9 million for sale listing (May 2009). 7,560 sq ft on 1.01 acres.
100 feet of waterfront, 5 bedrooms, 6.5 baths. Built in 1995.
Purchased in 2006 for $11 million.

From the Internet listing: "Magnificent 1 acre estate in Medina (10 min from Seattle) with approx. 100 ft. of low-bank waterfront with access to the ocean. Large dock with depth and space for a large yacht, complete with power, water, & lift. High-tech infrastructure throughout with a state-of-the-art entertainment system. Slate roof, copper gutters, blue stone slate covered terraces, hot tub, 4 car garage. Separate 500 sf guest house with fully equipped kitchen, bath, and fireplace. This property is total perfection."

This is our southern-most Medina home in Fairweather Bay. The Medina – Hunts Point border is at the south end of the bay.

Hunts Point
Powell, Peter – Powell Development

$8.5 million estimated value. 5,770 sq ft on 0.65 acres.
390 feet of waterfront, 5 bedrooms, 5.75 baths. Built in 2003.

This is the home of **Peter W. and Maryanne Powell**. Peter is President
of Kirkland-based Powell Development Co. The company develops and
constructs stores and retail shopping centers in five PNW states. It is
also a property manager.   It has developed and built stores for
Albertsons, Safeway, Fred Meyer, Walgreens, Costco, Lowe's and
others. Peter's father, Lloyd Powell, founded the company in the early
1970s.   Peter and Maryanne have donated generously to their alma
mater, the University of Oregon, and have established a Peter W. and
Maryanne L. Powell Distinguished Research Scholar award at the
University.

This is our western-most Hunts Point home and is near the end of
Fairweather Bay on a man-made peninsula. The Medina – Hunts Point
border is just northwest of the man-made canals on the south end of the
bay. Both canals are in Hunts Point.

$13 million estimated value. 12,430 sq ft on 2.16 acres.
158 feet of waterfront, 5 bedrooms, 5.25 baths.   Built in 1977.
Purchased in 1977 for $6 million.

This is the home of **David A. and Sandra Sabey**. David is the founder (1972), President and CEO of Tukwila-based Sabey Corporation. The $400 million company builds and leases data centers for the government and large corporations.   It also develops real estate and manages property. He has been called "the Donald Trump of Puget Sound." The couple is on the donor honor rolls for local hospitals and charities. They were honorary co-chairmen at the 1990 Seattle ball raising money for the American Cancer Society. He recently established the Seattle Science Foundation to establish an international communication network for the medical industry. The couple has contributed to both major parties.

Hunts Point Information
Fairweather Bay

$8.5 million estimated value. 7,100 sq ft on 1.46 acres.
110 feet of waterfront, 5 bedrooms, 4.5 baths. Built in 1975. Purchased in 1994 for $4 million.

Hunts Point's tip was acquired and named in the 1870s by Yarrow Point resident, **Leigh S. J. Hunt** (page 162), who owned the *Seattle Post Intelligencer*. He wanted to cut down the peninsula's trees that were obstructing his view of Seattle. The property was taken over by a bank around 1900 and sold to a group of Seattleites who used it as a retreat for picnics and camping. A community club house was built just north of here in 1913. At that time there was a small ferry to Seattle with a daily schedule. When it did not operate people would row to or from Seattle. The area's population grew after the first floating bridge (current I-90 location) was completed. Hunts Point was incorporated as a Fourth Class Town in 1955. The first sewer system was installed in 1960. Development began in earnest when the SR-520 bridge was completed in 1963. (Continued on page 140)

$9 million estimated value. 6,870 sq ft on 1.82 acres.
130 feet of waterfront, 4 bedrooms, 5 baths. Built in 2003.

This is the home of **Rhoady R. Jr. and Jeanne Lee**. Rhoady and his father founded Issaquah-based Lakeside Industries in 1952. The company is a state leader in asphalt paving. He is retired and his two sons are the CEO and the President of the company. It is one the state's largest private companies. Seattle University's Lee Center for the Arts opened in 2006 as a result of the family's generosity. The couple is a major supporter of the Seattle Symphony, Seattle Library, Seattle University and other charitable and arts organizations. The couple has contributed to Democratic candidates.

135

$9 million estimated value. 9,675 sq ft on 1.07 acres.
80 feet of waterfront, 4 bedrooms, 5 baths. Purchased for $4.5 million in 2001 and the existing house was replaced in 2003.

This is the home of **Rodney D. and Janice Olson**. Rodney and three partners founded Seattle-based WestCoast Hotels 1988 with the purchase of three Seattle Hotels, the Camlin, Roosevelt and the Vance. WestCoast grew to 19 hotels in 1999 and was acquired by Spokane-based Red Lion Hotels Corporation. The couple has contributed to Republican candidates.

$12 million sales price in 1998. 5,770 sq ft on 1.13 acres.
87 feet of waterfront, 6 bedrooms, 4.5 baths. Built in 1927.

This formerly was a Nordstrom family member's home. Seattle-based **Nordstrom, Inc.** was co-founded in 1901 by **John W. Nordstrom** (1871-1963) and **Carl F. Wallin**. John's parents died when he was a young boy and he emigrated from Sweden with $100 at the age of 16. The first store was a shoe store in Seattle called Wallin & Nordstrom. The second store was opened in Seattle in 1923 and John W.'s son, **Elmer** (1905-1993) was in charge of the opening. In 1928 and 1929 John W. and Wallin sold their shares in the company to Elmer and his brother, **Everett** (1902-1972). In 1930 the company name became **Nordstrom's** and in 1933 **Lloyd** (1920-1976) Nordstrom joined his brothers, Elmer and Everett, to run the company. In 1958 the company sold only shoes in 8 stores in Washington and Oregon. It expanded into apparel with the acquisition of Best Apparel in 1963 and changed its name to **Nordstrom Best**. (Nordstrom continued on page 143)

137

$9.5 million estimated value. 4,200 sq ft on 1.68 acres.
134 feet of waterfront, 3 bedrooms, 2.5 baths. Built in 1921 and renovated in 1980.

This is the home of **Kirby B. McDonald**. He purchased and became Chairman and CEO of Seattle-based Universal Services in 1987. The company specialized in food services and housekeeping for companies with remote, overseas locations. It became Universal Ogden Services in 1990 and was successfully sold in 2000. At that time it had operations in 44 countries and 900 jobsites. He is on the Board of Directors of Seattle-based Contact Prepared Response, Inc. The company provides services to police, fire and other emergency responders for crisis management and emergency preparedness. He is on the Swedish Hospital Board of Trustees. He is the son of **Stanley McDonald**, the founder of Princess Cruises, and the brother of **Laurie McDonald Jonsson** (page 101).

$11 million estimated value. 7,960 sq ft on 1.56 acres.
128 feet of waterfront, 6 bedrooms, 5.5 baths. Built in 1996.

This is the home of **Steven W. and Cathy Hooper**. Steve is a founding partner, along with other former executives of Microsoft and McCaw, of Ignition Partners of Bellevue. Ignition started in 1999 and invests globally in emerging communications, Internet and software businesses and has become one of the largest venture-capital companies in the Northwest. Prior to starting Ignition he was with **Craig McCaw** (page 153) for 18 years and was CEO of every major McCaw Company except Nextel. In the early 1980s Steve was part of the small McCaw team that recognized cellular communication's potential. Steve personally financed and helped raise $200 million taking McCaw Cellular public in 1987 as the first high-profile cellular company in the world. The couple has contributed to Republican candidates.

Hunts Point Information
Fairweather Bay

$9 million estimated value. 6,580 sq ft on 1.17 acres.
100 feet of waterfront, 4 bedrooms, 5 baths. Built in 1989 and renovated in 2007. The owner has contributed to Democratic candidates.

Hunts Point (Continued from page 134). The 2009 approximate statistics for Hunts Point are: 204 acres, 2 miles waterfront, 450 people, 207 housing units (almost one acre average), $3.8 million average assessed home value, and $250,000 average household income. The last two amounts are the highest in the state. The Town of Hunts Point web site claims the town is now "a first class Fourth Class Town."

Hunts Point's main peninsula has one road, Hunts Point Road, running the length to the estate on the end (page 147). All the main peninsula's waterfront homes face Fairweather Bay on the west and Cozy Cove on the east. The lots stretch 100 to 200 yards from the water to the road. The town has about 40 non-waterfront parcels south of the peninsula. Some of the waterfront estates have one or more full-time gardeners. After the Sabey's (page 133) 12,430 sq ft mansion was built in 1977 the town council has been restrictive on granting permits for large houses.

$9 million estimated value. 4,980 sq ft on 1.24 acres.
111 feet of waterfront, 4 bedrooms, 2.25 baths. Built in 1981.

The cities of **Medina** and **Clyde Hill** and the towns of **Hunts Point** and **Yarrow Point** are often lumped together as a "community" and are known as the "**Points Communities**." The respective approximate populations of the four cities and towns are 3,000, 2,900, 450 and 1,000. All are in the top ten cities and towns in the state of Washington in per capita and household income (page 144). Clyde Hill occupies the large hill to the south of Fairweather Bay and Cozy Cove and has no waterfront. All the cities are in the Bellevue school and fire districts. The Medina police department covers Hunts Point and the Clyde Hill police department covers Yarrow Point.

Ebsworth, Barney – Art Collector

$25 million estimated value. 9,420 sq ft on 3.28 acres.
300 feet of waterfront, 3 bedrooms, 4.25 baths. Built in 2003.

This is the home of **Barney A. and Pamela Ebsworth**. Barney is retired and a world renowned art collector. In 2006 he was trying to build an Ebsworth Chapel in Bellevue or Seattle but it met with community resistance. In 1959 at the age of 25 he founded St. Louis-based INTRAV, a pioneer luxury charter travel company, and he was CEO until it was sold in 1999 for $115 million. He had expanded INTRAV and started the Royal Cruise Line in 1971 and the Clipper Cruise Line in 1981. He founded his own investment company, Windsor, Inc. in 1979. He provided start-up capital for Build-A-Bear Workshop, Inc. in St. Louis and is Director Emeritus. The company is now nationally in stores and allows customers to customize teddy bears. The couple moved to Hunts Point after he retired, acquired this parcel and had this custom mansion built. The mansion houses one of the world's finest art collections that the couple started acquiring in St. Louis. 65 artworks of an undisclosed value were donated to the Seattle Art Museum in 2007. The gift was part the museum's 1,000 pieces, valued at an estimated $1 billion, received form multiple benefactors for its 2007 reopening. He is a SAM trustee. He has contributed to Republican candidates.

142

$9 million estimated value. 6,300 sq ft on 1.21 acres.
125 feet of waterfront, 5 bedrooms, 5.25 baths. Built in 1974 and renovated in 1987.

This is the home of **John N. and Sally Nordstrom**. John retired as Director of Nordstrom in 2006. The couple has contributed to Republican candidates.

Under the leadership of Lloyd W. Nordstrom and majority ownership of the Nordstrom family, the Seattle Seahawks were established as an NFL expansion franchise in 1976. Lloyd died that year and John N. was the family member in charge. In 1990 the Nordstroms sold the Seahawks to Ken Behring who sold the Seahawks to **Paul Allen** (page 64) in 1997.

(**Nordstrom** continued from page 137) In the late 1960s Elmer's two sons, **John N.** (1935-) and **James F.** (1940-1996) and Everett's son, **Bruce A.** (1933-) were running the company. In 1971 the company had $80 million in sales and went public with its stock. In 1973 the name of the stores became simply "**Nordstrom**." The company expanded into Alaska in 1975, California in 1978, the Northeast in 1988, Texas in 1996 and the Southeast in 1998. In 1999 trading of the stock moved from the NASDAQ to the NY Stock Exchange with the company name Nordstrom, Inc. and the ticker symbol JWN, in honor of founder John W. Nordstrom. (Nordstrom continued on page 146)

Per Capita Income Information
Sinegal, James – Costco

$12 million estimated value. 8,370 sq ft on 1.56 acres.
165 feet of waterfront, 4 bedrooms, 4.25 baths. Built in 1994.

This is the home of **James D. and Janet Sinegal**. This is their second home on our tour. The first is on page 108 along with the couple's information. James is the President, CEO and co-founder, with **Jeffrey Brotman** (page 98), of Costco.

Per Capita Incomes: The 2000 U.S. census showed **Hunts Point** average per capita income of $113,816 as highest in the state and the 4th highest in the nation for places with its population or more. The respective amounts and state ranks (for places with a population of 450 or more) for **Medina**, **Clyde Hill**, **Yarrow Point** and **Mercer Island** were $81,742, $78,252, $72,135 and $53,799, with ranks of 2, 3, 4 and 7. Mercer Island and **Bellevue** ($36,905) ranked 1st in the state for cities their respective sizes or larger. **Seattle**'s was $30,306 and the state of Washington's average was $22,711, the 12th highest of the 50 states.

$18 million estimated value. 7,180 sq ft on 1.85 acres.
259 feet of waterfront, 5 bedrooms, 7 baths. Built in 1990.

This is the home of **Scott D. and Laurie Oki**. Scott is the owner of Oki Golf and formerly was Sr. VP of sales and marketing with Microsoft. He was born in 1948 in Seattle. He joined Microsoft in 1982 and built the company's international operations. He was made VP of domestic operations and was a key player in the company's sales going from $100 million to $1 billion in the five years. He was overseeing 3,000 employees when he retired in 1992 and cashed in stock options for approximately $100 million. He started Oki Golf with the acquisition of a 350 acre parcel that was an 1800s coal and construction waste landfill on top of a hill overlooking Lake Washington and Puget Sound. Because of landfill waste the property was not suitable for home construction but he has turned it into The Golf Club at Newcastle, a nationally top rated, high-end public 36 hole golf course with a 44,000 sq ft clubhouse. A photograph of the site is on page 92. While it was being built in 1994 he purchased The Golf Club at Echo Falls near the north end of Lake Washington. Oki Golf now owns nine golf course clubs in the Puget Sound area.

He runs the Oki Foundation that has given millions of dollars to charities and non-profit organizations. He serves on more than 30 advisory boards and boards of directors including president, chair and co-chair positions. He has funded, founded and co-founded other foundations and organizations for hospitals, museums, children's sports, scouting, chess, Japanese-American causes and social ventures. The couple has contributed to Democratic candidates.

145

$7.4 million for sale listing (May 2009). 3,860 sq ft on 0.28 acres. 75 feet of waterfront, 3 bedrooms, 4 baths. Built in 1999.
This is the home of **James F. Jr. and Sally Nordstrom**.

(**Nordstrom** continued from page 143) The fourth generation is now in charge of the company. **James F. Jr**. (1973-), son of James F. Nordstrom, is EVP and President, Nordstrom Direct. **Blake W.** (1961-) is the current Nordstrom, Inc. President and **Erik B.** (1964-) and **Peter E.** (1962-) are Directors and EVPs; the three are sons of Bruce A. Nordstrom.

Nordstrom now operates in 28 states with over 170 stores and 2008 sales of $8.3 billion and 50,000 employees. The company is renowned for high quality, a wide selection of styles and sizes and highly motivated employees producing outstanding customer service. In 2008 the company was ranked 24th in *Fortune* magazine's list of "World's Most Admired Companies." Since going public in 1971 with an, adjusted for splits, IPO price of $0.25 per share the stock has split 7 times. The stock was trading in June 2009 around $20 per share.

The Nordstrom family is noted for philanthropy in the states and cities of all its stores. Since it started in Seattle and its headquarters are here, the Nordstrom name is on the walls, towers and buildings of many non-profits. These include: units and wings at Swedish Hospital and Children's Hospital and Medical Center, a recital hall at Benaroya Hall, and the Tennis Center at UW.

$22.8 million for sale listing (May 2009). 2.02 acres.
748 feet of waterfront. 270 degree views. Purchased with 6,860 sq ft house in 2005 for $17.5 million. The house was demolished in 2007.

This is the site of the former home of **Stan Sayres** (1897-1956) "**The Legend of Lake Washington**" and "**The Fastest Man Afloat**." He was selling and racing cars in northeastern Oregon in 1926 when he had his first experience with a power-boat. He purchased a wrecked 40 mph outboard engine racing boat and began racing, designing and building race-boats. He moved to Seattle in 1931 and in 1937 he bought a 91 mph racing boat that his wife named *Slow Motion*. Stan changed the name to *Slo-Mo-Shun,* often called *Slo-Mo*. Stan designed, developed and built new and faster *Slo-Mos*. He moved to Hunts Point in the 1940s and built a 6,860 sq ft house. The neighbors in this sleepy community "enjoyed" (?) the roar and 30 ft rooster tails of his trials and practices.

He set his first boat-on-water speed record of 160+ mph in 1950 on LW and continued to set new records, all on LW, with his last at 178.497 mph in 1952. After his first record he took *Slo-Mo IV* to Detroit and won the 1950 Gold Cup, boat racing's biggest prize. This was a big upset to the hydroplane establishment. Stan brought hydroplane racing to LW in 1951 as part of the **Seafair** (page 8 and 55) celebration. The first Seafair was in 1950 to celebrate the centennial of the first U.S.-European Seattle settlement. The 1951 race was the first U.S. hydroplane race west of Detroit and was a huge success. Stan became a local hero. The races are now a Seafair tradition. He received a lot of local backing for his racing against the Detroit establishment. *Slo-Mo-Shun IV* and *V* won the next four Gold Cups. Please see page 55 for the **Stan S. Sayres Memorial Park** known as the "**Sayres Pits**."

Cozy Cove – Hunts Point Information

$10 million estimated value. 7,460 sq ft on 1.2 acres.
157 feet of waterfront, 5 bedrooms, 5.5 baths. Purchased for $5.8 million in 2001 and the existing house was replaced in 2002.

This is the home of a real estate developer and property manager who owns numerous apartments in the Puget Sound area. He has contributed to Republican candidates.

This home is near the north-west end of **Cozy Cove** in Hunts Point with the town of Yarrow Point to the east. This is the center of three bays and coves of Medina, Hunts Point, Yarrow Point and Kirkland. Residents like the protected waters for their yachts and seaplanes.

Seaplanes in Cozy Cove and Fairweather Bay

$9 million estimated value. 6,750 sq ft on 1.13 acres.
111 feet of waterfront, 3 bedrooms, 3.25 baths.   Built in 1990.
Purchased in 2003 for $7.4 million.

This is the home of **Dr. Richard W. and Marilyn Herzberg**. She founded Bellevue-based Bureau of Education and Research (BER). BER provides staff development and training for educators in North America. It conducts seminars and produces audio and video materials. The family gives generously to theaters, museums, the Red Cross and numerous local charities. The couple has contributed to Republican candidates.

Hunts Point – Yarrow Point Information
Cozy Cove – Wetherill Nature Preserve

$9 million estimated value. 7,540 sq ft on 1.54 acres.
129 feet of waterfront, 4 bedrooms, 4.25 baths. Built in 1987.

The Hunts Point to Yarrow Point border is in the **Wetherill Nature Preserve** at the southern end of Cozy Cove. It is named after **Sidona and Colonel Wetherill** who acquired the property from her parents in 1927. In 1988 their daughters deeded 16 acres for the preserve which will remain a "natural habitat area."

Looking east across Cozy Cove – Nature Preserve on right

$8.9 million for sale listing (May 2009). 4,710 sq ft on 1.07 acres. 86 feet of waterfront, 5 bedrooms, 5 baths. Built in 1976. Purchased 3/9/2007 for $7.9 million.

From the Internet listing: "The imprint of traditionalism on the treasured shores of Hunts Point. Magnificent gated 1.07 acres of exquisite, manicured grounds; a gentle slope to the 86' of spectacular freshwater coastline. Incomparable, substantial moorage for float plane and yacht. The soft interior palette draws your attention forward to the drama of Lk Wash. French doors, deep-set millwork. Bay windows, chocolate hardwoods. Intimate meandering paths. Special rose-orange brick façade and pillars. 7 car garage parking."

This is the home of **Brian Marcinek**. Brian is a Principal and CFO of Eagle Investments LLC, a venture capital firm founded by Craig McCaw (page 153) in 1993. He is also on the boards of other McCaw firms. Brian is often quoted as a spokesman for the McCaw family. He was previously an investment banker with Chase Securities and a consultant with Andersen Consulting.

The McCaw Family

The world famous **McCaw brothers**, **Bruce** (1946-), **Craig** (1949-), **John** (1951-) and **Keith** (1953-2002) are the sons of **Marion and J. Elroy McCaw**.   The brothers were born in Centralia, WA where Elroy founded radio station KELA in the 1940s.   He began acquiring radio stations and one was WINS, for $60,000 down, in NY which he sold in 1962 to Westinghouse Broadcasting for $10 million.   He moved the family to a 20,000 sq ft former Boeing family mansion in the Highlands area north of Seattle.   One of Craig's high school friends was **Bill Gates** (page 118).   Marion and Elroy started the McCaw family legacy of philanthropy.

Elroy entered cable television and the sons worked as door-to-door salesmen and linesmen.   In 1969 Elroy suddenly died at home from a massive stroke and was found by 19 years-old Craig.   Elroy had continued wheeling and dealing and at the time of his death the estate was virtually bankrupt.   Craig graduated from Stanford in 1972 and took charge, and with his brothers, turned the family's Centralia cable company into McCaw Cable Vision.   In the early 1980s it was the 20th largest cable carrier in the U.S.

The McCaw brothers turned their attention to the fledging cellular phone industry.   Cellular system territory rights were being sold by the U.S. government via lotteries.   The McCaws won some lotteries and, using borrowed money, bought out other winners.   They were the visionaries and pioneers when the telephone industry was investing in landline infrastructure and technology.   They founded Kirkland-based McCaw Cellular Communications, Inc. in 1984.   In 1986 they sold the cable business for $750 million and bought MCI's wireless operations for $122 million.   McCaw Cellular went public in 1987 raising $2 billion.   In 1994, with Craig as CEO, McCaw Cellular was sold to AT&T for $11.5 billion.   Following the sale Craig's net worth was $2.6 billion and each of the brothers' was slightly less.

Keith (page 38) lived in Madison Park, **Bruce** lives in Medina (page 106), **Craig** lives in Hunts Point (next page) and **John** lives in Seattle and other locations.

$26 million estimated value. 15,810 sq ft on 4.3 acres.
327 feet of waterfront, 8 bedrooms, 10.5 baths. The main house was built in 1995 and the smaller guest-house on the south-water side was built in 1986 (see next page).

This is the home of **Craig and Susan McCaw**. It was purchased in 1999 from **Kenny G** (next page) in a private transaction. Susan is a former U.S. Ambassador to Austria.

The Craig and Susan McCaw Foundation had contributed millions of dollars to local and international causes. Their areas of interest are "reducing suffering, improving education and making the world a better place." Susan has served on the board of Team Read, a children's literacy group. The couple has contributed to Republican candidates.

Please see the previous page for the McCaw family story and Craig's cellular industry pioneering. Following the sale of McCaw Cellular to AT&T in 1994 the McCaw brothers founded NEXTLINK Communications which was not successful. The same year Craig and **Bill Gates** (page 118) formed Teledisc, a satellite communication company whose growth has been less than the founders projected. In 2003 Craig founded Kirkland-based Clearwire Corporation and he is Chairman. The company went public in 2007 raising $600 million and Craig retained a majority of the shares. The company provides portable wireless high-speed Internet service. The company is in 50 markets, with 450,000 customers, 2,000 employees and $80 million in annual sales. He has been listed by *Forbes* as one of the wealthiest people in the world with his 2008 net worth estimated at $2.3 billion.

153

Kenny G – Saxophonist

The value and numbers are included in the items on the previous page.
Guest house: 4,760 sq ft on 1.1 acres.
50 feet of waterfront, 2 bedrooms, 3 baths. Built in 1986.

An Internet site, *Virtual Globetrotting*, shows this as the home of Kenny G (Gorelick) but it is no longer his. This home is included in the estate that was sold to **Craig McCaw** (previous page) by **Kenny G**. He is a friend of the McCaw families and performs at family weddings and other events. It is rumored that he stays in this guest house when he is in the Seattle area. *Virtual Globetrotting* also shows him having a Malibu, CA compound on the oceanfront that he purchased from actor Leonardo DiCaprio in 1999.

Kenny G won the 1994 Grammy Award for Best Instrumental Composition *Forever in Love*. He is best known for his saxophone playing. He is the best selling instrumentalist in the world with over 70 million singles and albums sold. His album *Breathless* sold 12 million copies. *Songbird* was his first number one singles hit in 1986. His other popular singles include *Forever In Love, Sentimental, Silhouette* and *The Wedding Song*. He composes and writes most of his songs along with songs for others. He was born in Seattle and went to Franklin HS where he played in the jazz band and played on the golf team. He is now one of the top celebrity amateur golfers. On summer evenings when he lived here he would sometimes sit on the end of the dock and play his saxophone. His beautiful music would resonate throughout the cove.

$9.5 million estimated value. 4,175 sq ft on 2.09 acres.
160 feet of waterfront, 5 bedrooms, 4.5 baths. Built in 1923.

This is the home of **Steven A. and Connie Ballmer**. They purchased the estate in 1987 for $1.3 million and extensively renovated the buildings, but maintained their charm, in 1991. Steve is the CEO of Microsoft. He joined Microsoft in 1980 for a percentage of the company, a $50,000 annual salary and stock options. He was Microsoft's 24th employee (page 12) and first manager other than Gates and Allen. He is known as the most flamboyant of the three with his Microsoft stage appearances being featured on Internet videos. In the early years he headed several divisions, became President and COO in 1998 and was named CEO in 2000. He has been listed by *Forbes* as one of the wealthiest people in the world with his 2008 net worth estimated at $15 billion. The couple has given generously to numerous charities but has tried to maintain a low-key profile. He has given over $10 million to UW. He has contributed to both major parties.

Koss, Mike – Microsoft, Entrepreneur

$10 million estimated value. 8,090 sq ft on 2.26 acres.
152 feet of waterfront, 4 bedrooms, 5.25 baths. Built in 2000.

This is the home of **Michael C. and Debbie Koss**. Mike was with Microsoft from 1983 to 2002. He was Product Unit Manager and was the manager for Outlook. He is now working with Seattle-based StartPad which is a group of entrepreneurs, developers and students to support the startup community and Faves.com which is an Internet personal communication site. He has contributed to both major parties.

Looking southeast at the Wetherill Nature Preserve

Hunts Point
Lytle, Charles and Karen – Lytle Enterprises

$11 million estimated value when complete. 10,610 sq ft on 2.12 acres. 155 feet of waterfront, 3 bedrooms, 5.25 baths.

Charles S. and Karen Lytle purchased this lot and its previous house for $7.3 million 8/21/2006 and are replacing that house. The new house is nearly complete and has many features and a similar look of their larger Mercer Island home that is for sale. Please see page 46 for biographical and first home information. This appears to be their home for downsizing.

This is our southeastern-most house in Hunts Point. The Hunts Point to Yarrow Point border is at the Wetherill Nature Preserve at the southern end of Cozy Cove.

Yarrow Point
Remala, Rao – Microsoft
Schrempf, Detlef - SuperSonics

$10 million estimated value. 7,340 sq ft on 0.6 acres.
98 feet of waterfront, 6 bedrooms, 6.75 baths.
Purchased in 1999 for $8.5 million.

This is the home of **Rao V. and Satya Remala**. Rao was with Microsoft from 1981 to 2004 and was the company's first hire from India. He is from a tiny coastal village. He was a writer of the original code for Windows. The couple has a foundation in their name with over $7 million. The foundation is supporting hospitals in his home village in India. The home is artfully decorated with sandalwood idols of Hindu gods.

This is the former home of **Detlef and Marianne Schrempf** which they had built for them in 1994 and they sold in 1999 when they moved to their present home. Please see page 85 for that home and biographical information.

This is our southwestern-most house in Yarrow Point.

Yarrow Point Information
Zbikowski, Mark – Microsoft

$9.5 million 7/15/2008 purchase price. 8,580 sq ft on 0.61 acres.
115 feet of waterfront, 4 bedrooms, 5.5 baths. Built in 1998.

This is the home of **Mark J. and Donette Zbikowski**. Mark started with Microsoft in 1981 at the age of 25. He is one of many 1981 Microsoft hires from Harvard where he graduated and knew **Steve Ballmer** (pages 12 and 155). Mark was one of Ballmer's first recruits. He was one of the architects of MS-DOS, OS/2 and Windows NT. He left Microsoft in 2006 and is a lecturer at UW and a technical advisor to several companies. The Zbikowskis own another house (page 86) in Meydenbauer Bay that is for sale.

Yarrow Point received its name from **Leigh S. J. Hunt** (page 134 and 162) when he named his estate "Yarrow" from one of his favorite poems by William Wadsworth. Hunt was YP's first land speculator and began buying land and building an estate on the point in 1988. Development of YP was similar to that of **Hunts Point** (page 134). Yarrow Point was incorporated as a town in 1959. The current approximate statistics for the town are: 231 acres, 1.7 miles waterfront, 1,000 people, 400 housing units, $1.3 million average assessed home value, and $118,000 average household income.

159

Yarrow Bay Information

$9 million estimated value. 7,490 sq ft on 1.27 acres.
160 feet of waterfront, 4 bedrooms, 6.25 baths. Built in 2000.

The citizens of **Hunts Point** and **Yarrow Point** join together each year for a well-known small-town-style 4th of July celebration that began in 1976. The Yarrow Garden Club was founded in 1948 and has helped establish beautiful gardens throughout the town. Its members have helped beautify state-wide schools, arboretums and historical sites.

$9 million estimated value. 10,630 sq ft on 1.14 acres.
100 feet of waterfront, 6 bedrooms, 4.25 baths. Built in 2001.

This is the home of **Carl T. Stork**. Carl is President of Bellevue-based Ciconia & Co. LLC, a private investment firm, and a Principal of Florida-based Wyndcrest Holdings, LLC, a private investment and acquisition firm. In 2006 Wyndcrest acquired California-based Digital Domain and Carl served one year as interim CEO. The company produces visual effects for Hollywood films with the latest notable success *The Curious Case of Benjamin Button*. He was with Microsoft from 1981 to 2002. His last position was GM for Windows Hardware Strategy. He is one of several of this book's 1981 Microsoft recruits from Harvard where he received a BA in physics. He is part owner of the Seattle Mariners. He and his former wife, Judith Bigelow, have given millions of dollars to various charities and non-profits. There is a **Judith Bigelow and Carl Stork Room** at UW in recognition of their donations to UW. He has contributed to Republican candidates.

Thompson, Richard – Microsoft
Hunt, Leigh S. J. – Seattle Post Intelligencer

$17 million estimated value. 4,760 sq ft on 3.54 acres.
465 feet of waterfront, 3 bedrooms, 3.25 baths.   Built in 1900.
Purchased in 1999 for $11 million.

This is the home of **Richard R. and Jean Thompson**. Richard "Rick"
is Corporate VP of Zune with Microsoft. Zune is the company's digital
music and entertainment brand. He joined Microsoft in 1987 as Product
Manager for the Microsoft Mouse. In 1995 he was VP of the Microsoft
Hardware Division. In 2000 he left the company to join Go2Net as CFO
and VP Product Development. He rejoined Microsoft in 2002 to run the
Windows Client Extended Platform Division. He was VP of other
divisions prior to being promoted to Zune. He is a co-owner of both
Seattle Chocolates and Ferrari of Seattle.

This was the home of **Leigh S. J. Hunt** (1855-1933) (page 134 and 159)
who owned the *Seattle Post Intelligencer*. He lived here in the late
1800s and built the current house around 1900. The house is about 100
feet from the water behind the trees. The waterfront looks like a park but
is part of the 3.54 acre estate.

This is the tip of Yarrow Point, offering fantastic 180° views of Carillon
Point to the east, Kirkland's marina and downtown to the north and the
north Seattle area to the west.

162

Yarrow Point
Mathews, Michelle - Microsoft

$8.5 million estimated value. 10,990 sq ft on 0.78 acres.
180 feet of waterfront, 6 bedrooms, 5.5 baths. Built in 1940.

This is the home of **Michelle Mathews**. Michelle "Mich" Mathews is Sr. VP for Microsoft's Central Marketing Group. She is a spokesperson for the company and often quoted in the media. She leads the company's integrated marketing communication. In 1989 she started as consultant to Microsoft in the U.K. She joined the company in 1993 to lead its corporate public relations. Prior to joining Microsoft she was with General Motors. She has been a major contributor to the Seattle Symphony. She has contributed to both major parties.

This home faces Yarrow Bay which is the eastern-most of three bays or coves in this section of Lake Washington. This is our southeastern-most house in Yarrow Point.

163

Kirkland – Carillon Point – Yarrow Bay

The Yarrow Point to Kirkland border is at the east end of Morningside Park at the southern end of Yarrow Bay. The park is 7 acres of open space with a community dock. The YP Town Hall is adjacent to the north. In the 1950s developers proposed creating a small Venice-like community with canals to the east of the park at the south end of the bay. In the 1970s a consortium of government agencies scaled back development plans and established the area as "undisturbed wetlands."

This is the northeastern-most point of our tour. **Kirkland** is to the east and north. Kirkland has The Eastside's main commercial marina. Downtown Kirkland is adjacent and is reminiscent of California beach towns with many small shops and cafes. **Carillon Point** has a marina, office buildings, restaurants and a hotel. The restaurants provide valet boat parking. This is the site of an early 1900s and WWII shipyard. Development of the current complex began in the late 1980s. **Craig McCaw**'s (page 153) Clearwire Corporation is headquartered here.

Kirkland – Yarrow Point border and undisturbed wetlands

Carillon Point

Kirkland – LW cruise ship port

Background, Future Editions and New Books

Hundred Homes Publishing was founded in 2009. The business plan for the publishing company and the research for the first book began in the summer of 2008.

Lake Washington 130 Homes is our first book. A book with this format has never been printed in the United States or, to my knowledge, in the world. Prior to computers and the Internet a lot of public personal information was buried in archives. Now that this information is easily accessible, Internet sites are publishing public personal information along with satellite photographs and the location of people's homes. Traditional publishers have been slow to follow and continue to be very selective about the homes for which they publish pictures, location and personal information.

Hundred Homes Publishing is breaking traditions. We plan to publish a similar book for each United States waterway with more than 100 waterfront homes valued for more than $2 million each. Our next book will be about Newport Bay in Newport Beach, California. This bay is man-made with 21 square miles of water with numerous islands and waterfront homes. These are the homes of numerous Southern California's celebrities and elite.

In producing *Lake Washington 130 Homes* we relied entirely on public information. We will contact residents and homeowners for information for our next edition. We hope our readers will send us interesting information to include. We will continue our research. We will use all these sources for corrections and information about the estates' histories and the people who live or have lived there. The homes and their owners and residents are constantly changing. We will incorporate the changes. We plan on producing an updated version of this book in approximately one year and at least every two years thereafter.

We will be posting an update of the listings and sales of the homes in this book on our web page. This will be similar to the tables on page 170 and 171.

David Dykstra

Publisher, Author and Photographer
Hundred Homes Publishing
www.hundredhomes.net

LW Tour 130 Estates' Statistics

Rank[1]	Page	M$[2]	Wf Ft[3]	Lot Sq Ft[4]	Acre	Past or Present Owners or Residents
1	64	**150.0**	505	**56,660**	**9.55**	Allen, Paul G
2	118	**150.0**	475	50,050	5.15	Gates, Bill and Melinda
3	111	45.0	372	24,130	5.12	La Haye,(Peter [1940-1999]), Sandra
4	120	40.0	244	27,255	4.35	Shirley, Jon & Mary
5	38	35.0	240	19,840	1.81	McCaw, (Keith [1953-2002]), Mary K
6	112	35.0	310	13,160	5.34	Undisclosed
7	46	35.0	150	22,779	2.00	Lytle, Charles S & Karen E
8	88	33.9	527	15,160	1.89	Undisclosed.
9	59	32.0	160	13,636	1.67	Ben Leland Construction
10	97	30.0	115	19,570	2.04	Myhrvold, Nathan P & Rosemarie
11	21	30.0	248	16,880	1.79	Schultz, Howard D & Sheri
12	153	26.0	327	15,810	4.30	McCaw, Craig & Susan; Kenny G
13	94	25.0	302	19,040	1.32	Simonyi, Charles
14	142	25.0	300	9,420	3.28	Ebsworth, Barney A & Pamela
15	98	24.0	215	11,500	2.35	Brotman, Jeffrey H & Susan
16	57	23.9	255	17,780	1.37	Lazarus, Jonathan D
17	147	22.8	**748**	0	2.02	Sayres, Stan
18	37	20.0	160	13,300	1.00	Blume, Bruce & Anne
19	100	20.0	305	8,610	5.36	Reed, William G Jr and Victoria
20	31	20.0	60	7,010	2.59	Horowitz, Russell C
21	145	18.0	259	7,180	1.85	Oki, Scott D & Laurie
22	162	17.0	465	4,760	3.54	Thompson, Rick; Hunt, Leigh S J
23	40	15.8	120	9,200	0.46	Rose, Peter J & Patricia
24	48	15.0	120	15,400	0.88	Undisclosed
25	110	15.0	175	14,030	1.96	Grinstein, Gerald B; Sikma, Jack
26	102	15.0	198	13,040	1.92	MacLeod, Gary & Michela
27	95	15.0	175	12,560	1.31	Naveen, Jain
28	29	15.0	180	8,690	0.44	Selig, Martin
29	126	15.0	176	7,050	1.15	Mastro, Michael R & Linda
30	33	15.0	146	6,580	0.46	Ackerley, Barry A & Ginger
31	133	13.0	158	12,430	2.16	Sabey, David A & Sandra L
32	19	12.9	135	7,470	0.72	Briggs, Jack R & Carol P
33	129	12.5	113	6,610	0.96	Undisclosed
34	124	12.0	147	13,200	2.37	Undisclosed
35	43	12.0	132	10,580	1.18	Galanti, Richard A & Barrie
36	41	12.0	145	9,360	1.60	Undisclosed
37	144	12.0	165	8,370	1.56	Sinegal, James D & Janet

Bold = **Maximum**, *Italics* = *Minimum*, Underline = Median

LW Tour 130 Estates' Statistics

Rank[1]	Page	M$[2]	Wf Ft[3]	Lot Sq Ft[4]	Acre	Past or Present Owners or Residents
38	137	12.0	87	5,770	1.13	Undisclosed; Nordstrom former
39	92	12.0	280	5,350	1.87	Undisclosed
40	58	11.0	244	11,300	1.01	Glazer, Marsha; Leven, Bruce
41	47	11.0	180	10,930	1.17	Suddock, George S & Linda
42	157	11.0	155	10,610	2.12	Lytle, Charles S & Karen
43	83	11.0	183	10,210	2.10	Luger, John J & Donna
44	20	11.0	_136_	9,000	1.01	Maffei, Greg & Sharon
45	139	11.0	128	7,990	1.56	Hooper, Steven W & Cathy
46	44	11.0	210	7,960	1.25	Dillon, Eric E & Hollis
47	39	11.0	130	6,890	0.78	Undisclosed
48	52	10.4	96	8,911	0.72	Norris, John B & Monica
49	103	10.0	110	12,270	0.85	Maron, Dr. Howard & Mary
50	71	10.0	260	11,400	1.89	Undisclosed
51	121	10.0	124	10,710	1.45	Foster, Michael G Jr
52	36	10.0	100	10,390	0.72	Tong, Richard C & Constance
53	51	10.0	90	10,340	0.70	Undisclosed; Israel, Sam (1899-1994)
54	122	10.0	129	10,000	2.45	Gaudette, (Francis [1936-1993]), Doris
55	156	10.0	152	8,090	2.26	Koss, Michael C & Debbie
56	49	10.0	173	7,988	0.52	Undisclosed
57	148	10.0	157	7,460	1.20	Undisclosed
58	22	10.0	134	7,360	1.20	Moseley, Furman & Martha Reed
59	158	10.0	98	7,340	0.60	Remala, Rao V; Schrempf, Detlef
60	85	10.0	85	7,200	0.90	Schrempf, Detlef & Marianne
61	35	10.0	120	7,060	0.76	Robbins, Richard J & Bonnie
62	66	10.0	237	6,620	0.73	Chang, Michael
63	99	10.0	150	5,330	2.59	Neely, Diana
64	131	9.9	100	7,120	0.69	Undisclosed
65	32	_9.6_	63	7,990	0.44	Undisclosed
66	109	9.5	102	9,775	0.88	Stevens, Charles G & Delphine
67	107	9.5	92	9,450	0.70	Perry, Wayne M & Christine
68	159	9.5	115	8,580	0.61	Zbikowski, Mark J & Donette
69	82	9.5	267	5,460	2.67	Myhrvold, Cameron D & Linda
70	138	9.5	134	4,200	1.68	McDonald, Kirby B
71	155	9.5	160	4,175	2.09	Ballmer, Steven A & Connie
72	50	9.3	160	4,710	1.27	Undisclosed

Bold = Maximum, *Italics = Minimum*, <u>Underline = Median</u>

LW Tour 130 Estates' Statistics

Rank[1]	Page	M$[2]	Wf Ft[3]	Lot Sq Ft[4]	Acre	Past or Present Owners or Residents
73	161	9.0	100	10,630	<u>1.14</u>	Stork, Carl T
74	93	9.0	120	10,250	0.96	Pigott, Charles M &Yvonne
75	136	9.0	80	9,675	1.07	Olson, Rodney D & Janice
76	78	9.0	100	9,670	0.64	West, Richard G & Leslie
77	101	9.0	105	9,600	0.65	Jonsson, Lars H & Laurie McDonald
78	130	9.0	78	9,330	1.84	Undisclosed
79	61	9.0	210	8,170	0.94	Undisclosed
80	81	9.0	336	8,160	0.76	Undisclosed
81	123	9.0	172	7,780	1.71	Undisclosed
82	91	9.0	157	7,710	1.17	Hughes, Lawrence P & Mary
83	150	9.0	129	7,540	1.54	Undisclosed
84	160	9.0	160	7,490	1.27	Undisclosed
85	114	9.0	188	7,200	1.47	Guyman, Douglas E & Charlotte
86	42	9.0	160	6,990	0.88	Higgins, Frank M II &Magid
87	117	9.0	160	6,950	0.49	Whitsitt, Bob & Jan
88	135	9.0	130	6,870	1.82	Lee, Rhoady R Jr & Jeanne Lee
89	149	9.0	111	6,750	1.13	Herzberg, Dr Richard W, Marilyn
90	140	9.0	100	6,580	1.17	Undisclosed
91	28	9.0	60	6,422	*0.16*	Selig, Andrea
92	23	9.0	120	6,420	0.41	Diamond, Joel & Julie
93	143	9.0	125	6,300	1.21	Nordstrom, John N & Sally B
94	26	9.0	100	5,895	0.80	Alvord, Ellsworth C & Eve
95	62	9.0	190	5,850	1.24	Chase, Brad M & Judy
96	115	9.0	<u>140</u>	5,560	3.14	Ferguson, Hugh S
97	141	9.0	111	4,980	1.24	Undisclosed
98	30	9.0	153	4,020	0.59	Ragen, Brooks S
99	151	8.9	86	4,710	1.07	Marcinek, Brian
100	53	8.8	110	9,000	0.76	Undisclosed
101	127	8.8	134	7,365	0.63	Liddell, Christopher P & Patricia
102	73	8.8	210	7,360	1.17	Undisclosed
103	163	8.5	180	10,990	0.78	Mathews, Michelle
104	56	8.5	80	10,700	0.43	Naveen, Jain; Facq, Jean-Remy
105	76	8.5	100	9,150	1.00	Greenstein, Jeffrey I & Judith
106	134	8.5	110	7,100	1.46	Undisclosed
107	87	8.5	145	7,030	0.67	Burnstead, Frederick H & Joan
108	34	8.5	65	6,590	0.48	Sloan, Stuart M

Bold = Maximum, *Italics = Minimum*, <u>Underline = Median</u>

LW Tour 130 Estates' Statistics

Rank[1]	Page	M$[2]	Wf Ft[3]	Sq Ft[4]	Lot Acre	Past or Present Owners or Residents
109	132	8.5	390	5,770	0.65	Powell, Peter W & Maryanne
110	63	8.5	200	5,400	0.87	Schocken, Joseph L & Judith
111	70	8.0	95	8,400	0.62	Ferry, Richard
112	90	8.0	118	7,950	0.65	DiCerchio, Richard & Christine
113	89	8.0	155	7,190	0.60	Scott, J Lennox
114	72	8.0	175	6,880	1.47	Humphrey, David; Bonica, John J
115	24	8.0	120	5,570	0.51	Holmes, Dr King K Sr
116	128	8.0	119	4,970	0.70	May, Peter J & Patricia
117	86	8.0	85	7,420	0.69	Zbikowski, Mark J; Sikma, Jack
118	125	7.9	71	8,030	0.63	Knook, Pieter C & Anne
119	96	7.9	*42*	6,200	0.64	Undisclosed
120	116	7.8	115	6,320	0.73	Undisclosed
121	108	7.5	95	6,200	0.80	Sinegal, James D & Janet
122	113	7.5	106	6,080	1.48	Pigott, Mark & Cindy
123	60	7.5	195	5,290	0.49	Zorn, Jim
124	75	7.5	112	3,920	0.58	Blethen, Frank A Jr & Charlene
125	146	7.4	75	3,860	0.28	Nordstrom, James F Jr & Sally
126	27	7.0	120	5,220	0.68	Skerritt, Tom
127	68	7.0	147	5,150	0.63	Onetto, Marc A & Sally C
128	74	4.4	85	8,000	0.41	Lewis, Rashard
129	67	3.7	96	*3,670*	1.40	Holmgren, Mike & Kathy
130	54	*3.5*	85	3,880	0.43	Sasaki, Kazurhiro
Maximum		**150.0**	**748**	**56,660**	**9.55**	
Minimum		*3.5*	*42*	*3,670*	*0.16*	*(The vacant lot not included)*
Median		9.6	138	7,950	1.14	

Bold = **Maximum**, *Italics* = *Minimum*, Underline = Median

[1] Ranked by value, then sq ft, then acres.
[2] Million Dollars Value: (1st) If for sale (May 2009), listing price; or (2nd) recent sale-purchase price; or (3rd) cruise-by estimate, only if greater than (2nd).
[3] Waterfront linear feet.
[4] Square feet of living area. This is from public records which exclude garage space, boat houses, non-living dock houses and sheds, separate enclosed sports courts, and sometimes the indoor area (if it is not part of the living area) of indoor/outdoor pools.

May 2009 Listings

Rank[1]	Page	M$[2]	Wf Ft[3]	Sq Ft[4]	Lot Acre	Past or Present Owners or Residents
1	46	35.0	150	22,779	2.00	Lytle, Charles S & Karen E
2	88	33.9	527	15,160	1.89	Undisclosed
3	59	32.0	160	13,636	1.67	Ben Leland Construction
4	57	23.9	255	17,780	1.37	Lazarus, Jonathan D
5	147	22.8	748	0	2.02	Sayres, Stan
6	33	15.0	146	6,580	0.46	Ackerley, Barry & Ginger
7	19	12.9	135	7,470	0.72	Briggs, Jack R & Carol P
8	52	10.4	96	8,911	0.72	Norris, John B & Monica
9	85	10.0	85	7,200	0.90	Schrempf, Detlef & Marianne
10	131	9.9	100	7,120	0.69	Undisclosed
11	32	9.6	63	7,990	0.44	Undisclosed
12	151	8.9	86	4,710	1.07	Marcinek, Brian
13	53	8.8	110	9,000	0.76	Undisclosed
14	73	8.8	210	7,360	1.17	Undisclosed
15	127	8.8	134	7,365	0.63	Liddell, Christopher
16	86	8.0	85	7,420	0.69	Zbikowski, Mark; Sikma, Jack
17	125	7.9	71	8,030	0.63	Knook, Pieter C & Anne
18	96	7.9	42	6,200	0.64	Undisclosed
19	116	7.8	115	6,320	0.73	Undisclosed
20	146	7.4	75	3,860	0.28	Nordstrom, James F Jr & Sally
21	74	4.4	85	8,000	0.41	Lewis, Rashard

[1] Ranked by value, then sq ft, then acres.
[2] Million Dollars: (May 2009), listing price.
[3] Waterfront linear feet.
[4] Square feet of living area. See page 169.

Recent Sales[5]

Rank[1]	Page	M$[2]	Date	Wf Ft[3]	Sq Ft[4]	Lot Acre	Past or Present Owners or Residents
1	31	20.0	4/19/00	60	7,010	2.59	Horowitz, Russell C
2	147	17.5	12/15/05	748	6,860	2.02	Sayres, Stan
3	40	15.8	2/15/08	120	9,200	0.46	Rose, Peter J & Patricia
4	126	15.0	7/16/06	176	7,050	1.15	Mastro, Michael & Linda
5	33	13.3	6/11/08	146	6,580	0.46	Ackerley, Barry & Ginger
6	129	12.5	3/31/08	113	6,610	0.96	Undisclosed
7	137	12.0	7/31/98	87	5,770	1.13	Undiscl; Nordstrom former
8	131	11.0	8/22/06	100	7,120	0.69	Undisclosed
9	66	10.0	3/27/08	237	6,620	0.73	Chang, Michael
10	159	9.5	7/15/08	115	8,580	0.61	Zbikowski, Mark & D
11	50	9.3	8/14/08	160	4,710	1.27	Undisclosed
12	28	9.0	9/21/04	60	6,422	0.16	Selig, Andrea
13	151	7.9	3/9/07	86	4,710	1.07	Marcinek, Brian
14	128	7.0	4/26/06	119	4,970	0.70	May, Peter J & Patricia
15	68	5.6	7/3/07	147	5,150	0.63	Onetto, Marc A & Sally C
16	67	3.7	4/4/08	96	3,670	1.40	Holmgren, Mike & Kathy

[1] Ranked by value, then sq ft, then acres.
[2] Million Dollars: Recent sale-purchase price.
[3] Waterfront linear feet.
[4] Square feet of living area. See page 169.
[5] Sales-Purchases since 2004; earlier if within 10% of the estimated value; Transactions have been excluded when substantial construction occurred after.

Home Index – Alphabetical

Alphabetical – Home Index

Home Index – Page

Page – Home Index

Index

Index

Bibliography

America's Home Source; http://sea.themlsonline.com/

BlockShopper Seattle; http://seattle.blockshopper.com/

BNET; http://www.bnet.com/

City of Bellevue; http://www.ci.bellevue.wa.us/pdf/Finance/06-about_bellevue_budget_final_2009.pdf

Costco Wholesale Corporation; http://phx.corporate-ir.net/phoenix.zhtml?c=83830&p=irol-irhome

Forbes.com, The 400 Richest Americans; http://www.forbes.com/lists/

Gellatly, Judy. *Mercer Island Heritage*. Mercer Island historical Society, 1989.

Google; http://www.google.com/search/

Historylink.org, The Free Online Encyclopedia of Washington State History; http://www.historylink.org/

Huffington Post (The); http://www.huffingtonpost.com/ (political contributions)

King County; http://www.kingcounty.gov/

Knauss, Suzanne (editor). *A Point in Time, A History of Yarrow Point, Washington*. Belgate Printing, 2002.

Luxe, Volume II Issue I; http://www.luxemagazine.com/

McDonald, Lucille. *Bellevue – Its First 100 Years*. Bellevue Historical Society, 2000.

Microsoft Corporation; http://www.microsoft.com/msft/default.mspx

NNDB tracking the entire world; http://www.nndb.com/

Philanthropy Journal; http://www.philanthropyjournal.org/

Puget Sound Business Journal; http://www.bizjournals.com/seattle/

Real Estalker (the); http://realestalker.blogspot.com/

Seattle, City of; http://www.seattle.gov/

Seattlepi.com; http://www.seattlepi.com/

The Seattle Times; http://seattletimes.nwsource.com/html/home/index.html

Virtual Globetrotting; http://virtualglobetrotting.com/

Welch, Bob. *Bellevue and the New Eastside*. Windsor Publications, Inc. 1989.

White Pages (The Official); http://www.whitepages.com/

Wikipedia, The Free Encyclopedia; http://en.wikipedia.org/

Zillow.com; http://www.zillow.com/

About The Author

The author, David C. Dykstra, lives on Mercer Island waterfront and has extensively cruised, photographed and researched the lake and its waterfront estates. His previous books are *Computers For Profit* and *Manager's Guide to Business Computer Terms*. He has published numerous articles about computers and management information.

David earned a BS in Chemical Engineering degree from the University of California at Berkeley in 1963, an MBA degree from Harvard in 1966 and a California CPA license in 1977. In 1966 he started a career in accounting, finance and administration with Texas Instruments. His last major corporate position was Executive VP and CFO for TreeSweet Products Company in California. TreeSweet was a major U.S. producer of juice products that was later acquired (and its name disappeared) by NY-based Seneca Foods Corporation. In 1980 he started his own consulting firm in Newport Beach, California. He specialized in helping small and mid-sized business with their accounting and financial needs and converting to computer systems. He wrote numerous articles and two books based on his consulting experiences.

In 1994, after 25 years in Newport Beach, he came to the PNW on a consulting job and became a California to Washington State convert. David discusses his move and cruising background in the preface on page 6. Since retiring in 1999 he has become an accomplished photographer and has produced multimedia DVDs from his worldwide travels. In 2008 he started a publishing and writing career that is described on page 165.

David and his wife, Susan, on their Mercer Island deck